Who Dares Wins Publishing
445 Ridge Springs Drive
Chapel Hill, NC 27516

Electronic ISBN 9781935712855
Print ISBN 9781935712862

The ShelfLess Book
The Complete Digital Author
by
Bob Mayer & Jen Talty

TABLE OF CONTENTS

SECTION ONE: INTRODUCTION

With all the confusion going on in publishing, it comes down to this simple equation that has been ignored for decades in publishing (note how the Amazon exec says almost the same thing): Writers produce the product, readers consume the product. Everyone else is in between. At **Who Dares Wins Publishing** our motto is: Lead, follow or get the hell out of the way (http://whodareswinspublishing.com).

We prefer to lead.

Whether you have been published by a New York publisher, a small independent press, an ePublisher and are considering self-publishing or have never published and are considering all your options, this book has all the information you need to make informed decisions so you can be successful on whatever publishing path you choose to take. There are many roads to Oz.

We're starting this book with content and theory before we get into the nuts and bolts of producing and selling digital books. Similarly, your priority must always be writing and producing content, because you must have something to produce and sell.

We also repeat things. A lot. The reason for this is two-fold. As a Special Forces instructor, Bob learned the importance of repetition. Sometimes it doesn't sink in the first time. The second reason is we've learned repetition and consistency are key to success in digital publishing.

Bob Mayer and Jen Talty

DIGITAL HISTORY

For decades, the chokepoint in publishing was shelf space. There was only so much space in the bookstore for a limited number of books. This was the chokepoint and drove the entire business. Sales forces were not focused on selling books to readers, but rather getting distribution to consignment outlets.

With eBooks, publishing has undergone a radical change in business model that many people still do not quite grasp. Distribution is no longer the chokepoint, thus the ShelfLess Book, more commonly known as the eBook.

The electronic book has been around for more than a decade. The first eReader was the Data Discman, which was launched by Sony in 1992. The Data Discman read eBooks that were stored on CDs and the selection was limited to small specific groups, mostly technical and manual type books. It wasn't until the late 90s and early 2000s that digital books started to become popular, though again, being a very small portion of the market.

Bob remembers agent Richard Curtis launching eReads and holding up a mini-CD declaring it was the future of publishing. He was right, but perhaps too soon. The CD book never caught on, mainly because there was no popular hardware specifically designed for it.

In 2000, Ellora's Cave opened its doors as an erotic eBook publisher. We also saw Stephen King offer his book **Riding the Bullet** in digital format, but this book could only be read on your computer.

Random House and Harper Collins began selling digital versions of some of their English titles in 2002, and in 2004 we saw the very first eInk eReader: the Sony Librie. Other small ePublishers such as The Wild Rose Press and Samhain began taking submissions and publishing digital and print-on-demand eBooks, but the digital market share was barely 3% of the entire market as late as 2009.

The digital revolution began when Amazon bought Mobipocket in 2005. In 2006, the Sony Reader with eInk was introduced. The same year BooksOnBoard opened their doors and began selling eBooks in various formats. But the real fun began in 2007 when Amazon launched the Kindle in the US. However, few in publishing saw eBooks as a real contender in publishing. Traditional publishing is just that: steeped in tradition. Most large organizations are built on history, not foresight. This lack of vision in traditional publishing put many midlist authors who were already struggling in a very interesting position. Those who dared to think outside the traditional model and jumped full force into the digital revolution have opened many doors for all writers. In 2010 into 2011, it was considered radical for a traditionally published author to abandon their usual way of doing business and strike out on their own. We started Who Dares Wins Publishing in 2010, but Bob only made the 100% commitment to being independent in January of 2011. That month we sold 347 eBooks. By July of that year, we were selling over 100,000 eBooks a month.

Still, traditional publishing was fighting the digital revolution, holding on to their old business model, trying to keep their foothold in physical distribution, even when Borders went out of business. Even though one could see a template for what was happening by looking to the music industry, once a $12 billion a year business in 2000. The advent of Napster and downloads radically changed the distribution model. How many music stores are left in your town? Artists could also think in terms of single songs instead of albums with the advent of iTunes and the .99 download. Many music labels went under and the industry saw the rise of the indie musician who not only produced the product, but learned how to package it, market it, and sell it.

In 2008, Mark Coker launched Smashwords. Today, Smashwords is one of the leading online sites for the Independent author. Smashwords is a free site to the author, taking only a small portion of sales. Smashwords not only converts the Word document, it offers distribution to various major eBook retailers. In the coming year we will see many other sites similar to Smashwords, such as Vook, which Jen Talty had the privilege of beta testing. Vook will be made available in early 2012.

2010 and 2011 brought lightning fast changes to an industry that is notorious for being slow. Leading the way were companies like Amazon, which revolutionized the way the average reader purchases and reads books through the release of the Kindle. Barnes and Noble followed suit with the Nook. Apple developed the iPad and Kobo developed its own dedicated eReader as well. These companies listened to their customers. Amazon might be a giant, and perhaps publishers and many others view them as the enemy, but Amazon has always maintained their first loyalty is to their customer. Everything they do is about bringing the best product to their customer at the lowest price possible.

When Amazon opened up KDP (Kindle Direct Publishing) they gave the author (many of whom had been dropped or opted out of traditional publishing) the opportunity to connect with their readers by bringing back out of print books as well as continuing series that New York publishers had passed on. Publishing is a numbers business and when an author doesn't reach the publisher's desired selling rate, they are dropped. Before the Internet with online buying and before the age of digital books, this practice probably had more to do with readers' tastes. However, when the Internet began to compete with physical stores and the major chains began only stocking the top 10% of publishing, it became impossible for authors to reach the magic number. All that has changed with rise of The Digital Author.

The consignment method served a purpose in publishing for decades but unless a publisher committed to an author, it was the kiss of death for the midlist author. A common practice is for buyers for stores to order based on previous sales figures. Given that sales are consignment driven, this often meant that orders for subsequent books for authors were continually going lower, meaning fewer books were racked, meaning fewer books were sold, meaning the author's career was in a downward spiral regardless of the quality of the book. 90% of midlist authors experienced this and were eventually dropped by their publishers.

Barnes and Noble's PubIt has begun partnering with Independent authors. Bob Mayer was the first promotional partnership in Nook First and his release *The Jefferson Allegiance* soared to #2 nationally on the Barnes and Noble site as an eBook over Labor Day weekend 2011. Both Lisa Gardner and CJ Lyons hit the *New York Times* list with digital-only releases. They may have been the first, but they won't be the last.

Self-publishing used to be the ugly step-child of our industry, now it's all the rage. Everyone is doing it, but not everyone is doing it with the same results. Why? Because most authors are just putting their books up there, hoping to sell a few copies, spinning their wheels on social media sites and not focusing on all the aspects that go in to being successful business people. In the past, most writers thought the business of an author was to learn their craft and write better books; now the business of ALL authors includes marketing, promotion and selling. If you self-publish, then you add in the need to create the digital product and/or POD (Print on Demand) and get that product to your readers. Distribution is no longer the chokepoint. But discoverability is.

In this book we are going to talk about what goes in to successful self-publishing from the concept, to the book on the reader's device. The information we give is based on our collective thirty years in traditional, digital and self-publishing. We will start at the beginning and take you through the steps we have used to create Who Dares Wins Publishing. We will cover all the basics from planning how to publish, the steps to create a kick-ass product (it's not just in the writing, delivery counts for a lot), to how to get your product "out there" and discovered, and, finally, what we think the future holds.

MEET THE AUTHORS

NY Times bestselling author **Bob Mayer** has had over 50 books published. He has sold over four million books, and is in demand as a team-building, life-changing, and leadership speaker and consultant for his *Who Dares Wins: The Green Beret Way* concept, which he translated into Write It Forward: a holistic program teaching writers how to be authors. He is also the Co-Creator of Who Dares Wins Publishing, which does both eBooks and Print On Demand, so he has experience in both traditional and non-traditional publishing.

His books have hit the *NY Times, Publishers Weekly, Wall Street Journal* and numerous other bestseller lists. His book *The Jefferson Allegiance,* was released independently and reached #2 overall in sales on Nook.

Bob Mayer grew up in the Bronx. After high school, he entered West Point where he learned about the history of our military and our country. During his four years at the Academy and later in the Infantry, Mayer questioned the idea of "mission over men." When he volunteered and passed selection for the Special Forces as a Green Beret, he felt more at ease where the men were more important than the mission.

Mayer's obsession with mythology and his vast knowledge of the military and Special Forces, mixed with his strong desire to learn from history, is the foundation for his science fiction series *Atlantis, Area 51* and *Psychic Warrior.* Mayer is a master at blending elements of truth into all of his thrillers, leaving the reader questioning what is real and what isn't.

He took this same passion and created thrillers based in fact and riddled with possibilities. His unique background in the Special Forces gives the reader a sense of authenticity and creates a reality that makes the reader wonder where fact ends and fiction begins.

In his historical fiction novels, Mayer blends actual events with fictional characters. He doesn't change history, but instead changes how history came into being.

Mayer's military background, coupled with his deep desire to understand the past and how it affects our future, gives his writing a rich flavor not to be missed.

Bob has presented for over a thousand organizations both in the United States and internationally, including keynote presentations, all day workshops, and multi-day seminars. He has taught organizations ranging from Maui Writers, to Whidbey Island Writers, to San Diego State University, to the University of Georgia, to the Romance Writers of America National Convention, to Boston SWAT, the CIA, Fortune-500, the Royal Danish Navy Frogman Corps, Microsoft, Rotary, IT Teams in Silicon Valley and many others. He has also served as a Visiting Writer for NILA MFA program in Creative Writing. He has done interviews for the *Wall Street Journal*, *Forbes*, *Sports Illustrated*, PBS, NPR, the Discovery Channel, the SyFy channel and local cable shows. For more information see www.bobmayer.org.

Jen Talty co-created Who Dares Wins Publishing with *NY Times* Best-Selling Author Bob Mayer, and runs the technical side of the company. She is a published romance author, and teaches Creative Writing at various writing conferences across the country.

Jen grew up in Rochester, NY, a city with the highest murder rate per capita in the entire state. With notorious cases such as The Alphabet Murders, The Genesee River Killer (Arthur Shawcross), The

Murder of Kali Ann Poulton by Mark Christi, and the case of funeral homes stealing body parts from corpses awaiting cremation, Jen became fascinated by the darker side of human nature. She brings this fascination to her romances, creating dark villains who wreak havoc on the hero and heroine, and producing page-turning suspense.

Jen received a BS degree in Business Education with a concentration in Marketing and Sales from Nazareth College of Rochester. She taught Business Applications at both the high school level and in Continuing Education. She was a co-leader of Distributed Education Clubs of America and worked with students in developing marketing, sales and public speaking skills. After leaving the teaching profession, she worked as a product and sales trainer for various hardware and software companies such as 3Comm, HP and McAfee, and was the regional merchandising representative for Buena Vista Entertainment.

Who Dares Wins Publishing was formed as a vehicle to launch Bob Mayer's backlist into digital publication. It was built on the notion that **writers produce the product, readers consume the product and everything else is in between.** The 21st century has brought the rise of the digital author. It is time to take control.

Write It Forward (http://writeitforward.wordpress.com), a division of Who Dares Wins Publishing was formed because both Bob Mayer and Jen Talty believe the two most important people in the publishing business are the *writer* and the *reader*. The key to being successful in a business where 99% of what is submitted or self-published is rejected or fails is education and understanding. *Write It Forward* is dedicated to giving writers the tools and information they need to increase their chances of success. It truly is a great time to be an author.

THE ULTIMATE GATEKEEPER: YOU, THE AUTHOR

In the past, we always thought of Agents and Editors as the gatekeepers between writers and their potential readers. These people decided which writers got read and which writers received standard rejection letters. They alone decided which authors would be presented to the buyers of bookstores and finally placed in the readers' hands.

The rise of the Digital Author has given many writers the ability to connect directly with their readers. It is the Reader who decides if they are going to take a risk on a book and if they are going to buy another book from same author. It is the Reader who will make our careers. Without them, we don't exist. However, is it the reader who is the keeper of the gate, or the writer?

Ultimately, the true gatekeepers in 21st century publishing are writers.

We hear the screams. What about Agents? Publishers? Bookstores? The aliens from Roswell? That single book buyer for Wal-Mart?

Let us explain.

For many years the choke point in publishing was distribution. That's no longer true with the rise of eBooks and digital distribution. So the traditional route of *writer – agent – editor – publisher – sales forces – book buyer -bookstore – reader* has been broken. This is a good thing for the two people who matter most: the writer and the reader, because now there is a direct link between the producer and the consumer.

Readers are very smart people and they are capable of letting authors know what is good and what isn't. We really don't need editors and agents to tell us that. Actually, for the most part, editors and agents don't tell us it's not good, they tell us whether the publishers can distribute it. But who are the publisher's customers? The bookstore. And where are the bookstores going? Read our post on Starbucks (http://writeitforward.wordpress.com/2010/11/01/where-goes-starbucks-thee-goes-the-plan-for-bookstores).

Here's the deal: writers create the product. The quality of the product is going to determine how readers react to it. The ability to promote/market the product is going to determine if readers even get a chance to react to it.

So it's actually the writer who is going to determine his or her own success or failure. One thing to understand is that gaining national branding at the level of James Patterson is very difficult for the indie author; however, if we focus on our niche, our specific readers, we can create the necessary word of mouth that does sell books, and the bigger the word of mouth, the bigger we become.

99.5% of indie/self-published authors will be gone in two years. It's just a hard truth we have to face. They will step away, for whatever reason, and another indie will take their place. And be gone in two years. The gatekeeper to a writer's success is the writer and his or her own perseverance, talent, and willingness to learn and change. We have to keep producing quality books that our readers want to read and in turn will pass on to other readers. We have to continue to hone our craft. Learn from each other. We also have to continue to build our business and promote. Another mantra at Write It Forward is **Content is King and Promotion is Queen: together they rule the publishing world.** Today, you really can't afford one without the other.

The one thing that the indie writer does not have that is still in the hands of traditional publishing is placement. We will discuss this later, but it's important to understand that while the bookshelf space is no longer finite, the promotional placement and top 100 lists are. This doesn't mean an indie can't get attention...Bob Mayer, Amanda Hocking, J.A. Konrath...are all well-known indies who have had some help with placement. Whether it be through luck (having the *Area 51* cover be featured in new science fiction releases), networking and having conversations with decision makers (meeting with executives at conferences and having *The Jefferson Allegiance* featured on the B&N Nook blog during the first week of the release, launching it to #2 on the Nook national best seller list), or utilizing pricing strategies and studying the way Amazon works to have books break in to the top 100 lists in their category, it is possible to have success in indie publishing

11

if we take responsibility. One thing to consider is that Amazon currently does not allow paid placement for books on its site. It focuses placement and promotion on books that sell.

As authors we need to take responsibility for the quality of the words on the page and the quality of the general reading experience. An eBook is a tricky thing and it doesn't matter how good the book is; if the reader is dissatisfied with the reading experience, they won't come back for more.

As the technology gets better, the platforms adjust and the way eBooks are created adjusts. This means we need to keep remaking eBooks. Yes. It does. We recently saw a bunch of emails go out on an indie loop about some adjustments Nook must have made, as their eBooks now look different. This happened on Kindle a while back when we fixed a problem in all our eBooks, and while it looked great on Nook and iPad, it created a different kind of problem for the Kindle.

We have heard from our readers and we have responded by doing our best to make the necessary changes to make the reading experience the best possible. One thing we did consider, that many did not, was end matter and how much to put back there. Just because it doesn't cost any more to add excerpts from other books and advertisements, doesn't mean it's a good idea. When you read on an eReader it tells you the percentage to the end. If you get to 65% and the book stops, readers get upset because the rest is all promo. Even if they received an entire book at 100,000 words, they still feel short-changed in their expectations. We work at making sure our books go to at least 92%, but preferably 95% to hit THE END. We put a short list of books, and a couple page excerpt in our end matter. Any more than that, and you run the risk of upsetting the reader. We control this when we self-publish. But if a publisher is doing it, you don't control it and we have seen publishers pushing other authors and putting too much at the end of the book.

What you need to understand is that this issue with front and end matter is just being brought to light. Many people were thinking that adding all these "extras" was great promo and actually benefiting the reader. They thought they could hook the reader with another book. And it is great, but in moderation.

There is another argument that traditional publishing gives authors quality editing. Yes. It's true. They do. But in turn we've heard many a talented, established, multi-published author complain about the quality of their editors, or how they have to fight for what they know is best for their books and their readers. An indie author can contract out editing, often to the same people that traditional publishers contract. Regardless of the route, you will need to have your book edited, and you will need to take responsibility to do what is best for your book and for your reader.

Here is the deal: Anyone can self-publish, but only those who take responsibility will succeed.

Here are trends we see that will determine the few who get through the gate and find success:

1. **In it for the long haul, rather than thinking you're playing the publishing lottery.** We see far too many writers who want success now. They check sales figures every day. Instead, they need to think about perhaps succeeding in 3 to 5 years, with at least a half dozen titles under their belt.

2. **Plan for the long haul.** At Who Dares Wins Publishing we're always looking at least three years ahead. We have a writing and production schedule laid out that keeps us on task.

3. **Stay one step of ahead of the trends.** Act, don't react. This means sometimes you must take risks. Some of these attempts will fail, but the ones who succeed will be on the front end of the trends.

4. **Write good books.** This one seems so basic, but we see too many writers spend so much more time worrying about promotion than worrying about the quality of their craft. Bob has learned more in the last two years about writing than in his first twenty.

5. **Sweat equity.** This ain't easy. Never has been. We've watched the careers of many writers. The majority of writers who are having the most success as indies have a backlist, which is the sweat equity from the time they spent in the trenches in traditional publishing. If you don't have backlist, your sweat equity begins now.

6. **Run an efficient business.** Most writers just want to write. They don't want to deal with all the details of running a business, but being an indie author means you are self-employed. We know people who were great doctors or lawyers but went bankrupt because they couldn't run their own business.

13

7. **Networking and team building.** "Indie" is an interesting term because in fact, we believe it's very difficult to succeed on your own. You're going to need help with the books (editing, covers, formatting, etc.) and you're going to need help with the promoting.

8. **Build a platform that has a specific message.** At *Write It Forward* we view our platform as author advocate. We see too many writers whose platform seems to be "buy my book." People need a reason to read your blog, RT your tweets, and listen to you. The key to successful platform building and branding is the ability to create a community. It is not about selling, but making yourself available to those individuals who will be most likely to buy your books. Always be real and genuine.

9. **Stay informed.** Things are changing fast. Many people are trying a lot of different things. Some will work, some will fail. But staying up to date on everything that's happening can help you make informed decisions. Some things you can do for this are get on Kindleboards and follow and get involved in the discussions there as well as promote your book in the Book Bazaar forum. Subscribe to Publisher Weekly's Lunch and Deals for $20 a month. Stay active on Twitter and follow people who are knowledgeable about the business.

10. **Be assertive but not obnoxious.** We've grown much more assertive in the past six months. One of the largest mistakes Bob made coming out of Special Forces and going into traditional publishing was trusting that other people would do their jobs without having to look over their shoulders. This cost Bob. Now he pushes others, gently, but consistently, in order to achieve goals. No one cares more about the success of your book than you do. Always remember that. Perseverance and persistence count for a lot.

11. **In sum.** Writers, your fate is in your hands now.

CHANGES IN WRITING AND PUBLISHING

We are in the business of writing AND the business of publishing. We must master both aspects in order to succeed and that is true regardless if you self-publish or traditionally publish. You will hear over and over again from us that the best promotional/marketing tool you have in your arsenal is *writing good books*. One of the things we discuss in this book is techniques for building a marketing presence. One of the keys to this is the promise you make to your readers.

We don't believe in writing to the market, but it is important to look at the market and figure out where your book fits. The bigger the marketplace, the more important it is to be narrow. Find YOUR readers. Niche is key because niche is the foundation that you can build from. If you fulfill the promise to your readers, then your readers will tell others. That is how we sell books.

As time changes, so does reader demand. The great American classics, if submitted today to publishers, might be rejected. Basic novel structure has not changed, but writing styles over the years have changed as authors have pushed the envelope and taken risks.

The ability to update books with little cost has exposed readers to out-of-print books that aren't considered classics and breathed new life into many authors who were considered washed up by New York.

Bob wrote his first draft of *The Novel Writer's Toolkit* in 1994 after having four books published. It was all of eleven pages long. That was the extent of what he consciously knew about writing a novel. *Writers Digest* originally published the book in 2003.

In 2009, he wrote his first draft of **Write It Forward (originally titled *Warrior Writer*)**, a book designed to teach writers how to succeed as authors after his frustration over the lack of education for writers and all his experiences. Bob still has not had a single response from an agent or editor showing him what their formal training program is for an author they sign or contract. Neither has Jen over the last few years as she sent query after query, and many agents expected her to write up a marketing/promotion plan, yet they had no plan to train her in the business of publishing. In today's fast moving marketplace, writers can't afford to learn like Bob and many other traditionally published authors did — the hard way, by trial and error. This is not only inefficient, it can also be a career ender for an author.

We updated both books extensively in 2011, partly because we've grown as writers and now as independent authors. But also because today's publishing environment has changed, and with that change has come the ability to update books to meet the changing needs of today's successful writers. *The Novel Writers Toolkit* now focuses 100% on the craft of writing. Bob has added what he has learned during his writing partnership with Jenny Cruise, along with new techniques he's developed over the last few years.

We removed the business section in *The Novel Writers Toolkit* because that belongs in the other book: *Write It Forward: From Writer To Successful Author.*

The ability to update material is one of the great things about digital publishing. But it's also a problem because we've got to ask ourselves when is the right time to update? We spend a lot of time discussing the need to "keep pushing forward." If we are constantly updating books, when are we ever going to write new books? In order to build your niche, your readership, you need to write new books. We had been discussing updating these two books for about a year before we actually did. Why? In part, time. Bob was writing *Duty, Honor, Country A Novel of West Point and The Civil War*, and Jen was focusing her attention on loading backlist books to various platforms. What pushed us to make the changes was when we changed the title of Warrior Writer to Write It Forward. It made sense to make the updates at that time.

One key thing we added in the Toolkit was a section on Conflict, especially the Conflict Box. We have to be willing to grow and change in order to stay in the *business of writing* and the *business of publishing* long term.

In the Toolkit, Bob teaches how to answer key questions about your book. Because your book is the number one marketing and promotional tool you have, take the time to consider these questions. Write them down, then keep them at your desk when you are writing.

Can you state what your book is about in one sentence?

Do you clearly have conflict lock between protagonist and antagonist?

Do you know where your 'camera' is when you write each scene? i.e. Point of View? Do you know when you've done a cut (shift point of view)?

Do you know all your characters' primary motivations, their motivation levels, and their blind spot?

In a nutshell, we've continued to learn and grow as writers.

For decades, publishing remained the same. Authors wrote books, submitted, got agents, publishers bought books, distributed to bookstores (on consignment) and the author went back to their office to write more books, not thinking about the one being published. It was a luxury, but one that ended back in the early 90s when the Mass Market paperback crunch began and shelf space became very limited. Very few people saw the writing on the wall as the digital era began. Instead of acting, everyone in publishing was reacting to these changes, and most authors in Bob's position during the late 90s were in panic mode as print runs got smaller, the sell-through got higher and advances were dwindling.

It wasn't just that major retailers were only buying "name brand" authors, but changes in technology were already affecting the book buying experience. Things were beginning to go on-line and go digital. We all know what happened to the music business, but no one wanted to believe it would happen to the publishing industry. So when music went from a 12 billion dollar a year business in 2000 to a 6 billion dollar a year business in 2010, no one in publishing paid attention.

In the early 2000s digital publishing was on the rise. Many first time authors were turning to publishers like Ellora's Cave; however it had the stigma that it was only erotic titles, and it was viewed as not any different than self-publishing. The birth of the Kindle changed that, but no one in publishing wanted to believe it.

The following is a blog post that Bob published on November 9, 2010 titled **Resistance is Futile: The Future of Publishing.** Read the post, keeping in mind it was published in 2010 and a lot has changed...but has New York really changed?

Resistance is Futile: The Future of Publishing: A Write It Forward Blog Post

The Borg are in close Earth orbit and preparing to land. The future of publishing is now. I was recently speaking with a science fiction author. He also does consulting in the corporate world, except he doesn't call himself a science fiction writer when he does that; he's a futurist. And the #1 thing he preaches is that change is occurring exponentially, not linearly.

I have mentioned that publishers might well be 'juking the stats'. Publicly announcing 10% e-book sales, while every author I talk to who has actual numbers says it's between 40-60% overall. PW just announced John Grisham's latest release has significantly fewer hardcover sales, but it was also released in e-book. My latest royalty statement for my first Area 51 book showed e-book sales were double my mass market sales. I believe the Borg are checking those books out to determine whether I am an enemy or ally and how much I know about the Mothership. It's actually pretty cool.

Here are some facts:

The Big 6 Publishers control 95% of print publishing.
Starting in 1995, the print business began contracting.
7 out of 10 books printed by the Big 6 lose money.
10% of their titles generate 90% of their revenue.

Those two facts indicate a reality: the focus for the Big 6 is going to be more and more on the Brand Name authors and less on midlist. The problem is: where is the next generation of Brand Name Authors going to come from?

The decline of the book chains is the biggest problem for traditional publishers.

Here's the conundrum that NY doesn't want to face: The book business is the same, but the retail business has changed. While NY basically operates the same, the way books are sold has changed dramatically.

The focus is too much on celebrity books in NY and many are money-losers. Much more so than all those midlist authors. The bestseller lists are very deceptive. For example, Kate Gosselin's book sold only 11,000 copies yet hit #6 on the NY Times list. Someone is playing with the numbers to make it look good, but many of those big deals are money-bleeders for trad publishers.

The overhead for the Big 6 operating out of the Big Apple is way too high. Heck, even Who Dares Wins Publishing, which we started up in 2010 and operates out of my bunker in my house (lined with aluminum foil so the Borg can't read my thoughts) and Jen Talty's office in her house, has overhead. We could never operate brick and mortar out of a NY office. So that's something that's going to have to be addressed. I see further major contractions occurring in NY and more out-sourcing of jobs to people digitally. The acquiring editors will still be in NY with the agents, but a lot of the other parts are going to be out-sourced.

There are two major trends in publishing going on right now:

1. Mid list authors going it on their own. Actually, this is creeping upward. David Morrell (not a midlist author, can we say Rambo?) announced he is bringing nine books from his backlist into print AND his newest title on his own, skipping traditional publishing altogether. This is the biggest name fiction writer to do this (since this blog post can you say Pottermore?). So far. The perception right now is that overall, the quality of self-published books is poor. The reality is, most new authors who have self-published are indeed putting up poor quality. However, there are a number of traditionally published authors who are bringing backlist into print and these are books that have hit bestseller lists. Readers will separate the quality out.

2. Digital publishing is exploding. I've seen it just this year (2010). In January, there were many yawns at the Digital Book World conference. Those yawns have changed to expressions of shock. I've been predicting that the change from print to digital would be many times faster than most were predicting and I've been proved right (slight pat on the back). I predict by the end of

2011 we will be close to 50-60% of all books being digital. Especially with all the new e-readers that will be under Xmas trees next month (BTW, the Borg don't do Xmas).

The problem is this: the makers of digital platforms like Kindle and iPad want content. The Big 6 are loath to give digital content to them because they believe it cuts into their hardcover and other print sales and would hurt their own business. So there is a huge divide between the platform makers, primarily Amazon and Apple, and the content providers.

This is the VOID that will destroy some of the Big 6 if they don't exploit it. And also the VOID which savvy writers can fill.

Adapt or die.

It has been a while since that blog post was published and not much has changed with New York Publishing. Print publishing is still controlled by the Big Six, but Borders has closed and B&N physical shelf-space is still shrinking. While Amazon has entered the print business, indies are loath to stock them. But even more important, readers are buying more and more eBooks and soon we will see another major shift where eBooks will make up 80% of the market and print books will shift to POD across the board and make up maybe 20% of the business.

One thing to consider is EBM or the Espresso Book Machine. This machine allows customers to print whatever book they want. Imagine going into your local grocery store, dropping off your prescription (you have to wait at least 20 minutes), ordering a book at the EBM stand, and then do your grocery shopping. By the time you are at the check out, your prescription is ready and so is your next favorite book. Might as well hit the RedBox on the way out the door! Here is an interesting YouTube video about the Espresso Book Machine (http://youtu.be/Q946sfGLxm4).

Adapt or die. Authors and readers are adapting...bookstores are going out of business...publishers will have to change...so will agents. Right now, at Who Dares Wins Publishing, 99% of our fiction sales aree eBooks. Non-fiction, the ratio is roughly 50-50% but that includes a lot of hand-selling at conferences.

What does all this mean? It means that right now new authors and midlist authors have an opportunity they never had before. New York is going to continue to focus on the top 10% and the Big Six will adapt, but until that happens, the indie author has an opportunity to create a strong following so that when publishing does shift and New York finally turns their sinking ship around, the indie author will be in a position to survive and thrive in the future. The key is two-fold: *planning* and *execution.*

We will talk about goal setting in the next section, but take a moment to think about your goal and think about what is the worst thing that can happen and what is the best possible outcome. Understanding both ends of the spectrum will give you an added edge.

When we first started Who Dares Wins Publishing our worst-case scenario was we wouldn't make any money, best case, we'd break Bob out. Now, two years into it, we've learned many lessons, have adjusted our plan, and are working toward breaking Bob out (by the way — we exceeded by double our year end sales goal for 2011 in July 2011).

Recently Sourcebooks made a statement about how they have found a way to manage the making of an eBook and the digital distribution that will help them reduce costs and redundancy. They talked about advances in technology with InDesign and Word. Great for them, but what they are doing is what small ePublishers have been doing for many years and it's exactly what Who Dares Wins Publishing has been doing for the last 2 years. The New York publishers have to first recognize what needs to be changed and then implement those changes. It's going to take time for them to catch up. Also consider the reality that there are people embedded in those companies who are fighting the changes because it means they will lose their jobs in the new publishing paradigm.

This business is changing fast. It's not just the technology, like the new KindleFire, but what's key is how authors, agents, publishers etc. are adapting to these changes. We are seeing agents becoming publishers. We are seeing authors becoming publishers. We are seeing editors looking at the top 100 Amazon lists looking for the self-published author that is making a dent and offering them a book deal.

Above, we made a bold prediction about eBooks becoming 80% of the market. We believe that statement to be true, but we just don't know if that will happen in 1, 3, 5 or 10 years. No one knows what is going to happen. For all we know in five years we could be pushing our shopping carts down *The Road.* If that is the case, then everyone will need to read our planned book for 2012: *The Green Beret Guide To*

Surviving the Apocalypse, Zombies and Other Lesser Disasters. Again, this brings us back to *planning* and *execution.*

But the other thing we are seeing is the issue of placement, which you can also call "discoverability." It's much harder for the indie author to get product placement (what used to be co-op space in bookstores) for their books so readers can find them. If they can't find you, they can't read you.

Something else to consider in indie publishing is the time from idea to bookstore. In traditional publishing it's roughly three years from idea to bookstore. You have to write the book (a year) sell the book (a year) and go through production (a year). In indie publishing you have to write the book (still maybe a year, though Bob can write three books a year), then find beta readers and editors (that can be done in a month). Then make edits, and get a copy editor (maybe another month). Cover, file conversion and upload. At Who Dares Wins Publishing we can do that in two weeks depending on Jen's current workload. The question for traditional publishing is will they be able to publish faster given that the technology now supports a much quicker process? Considering that gaming companies, which know the technology, still take three years to produce a game, we're not sure.

It's never a good idea to write to the market, but it is important to watch for trends. Even more so now since we do have the ability to produce quality eBooks faster than traditional publishers.. But the key is quality.

The bottom line is you have to continue to learn your craft and you have to continue to learn your business and stay abreast of all that is going on around you. A mantra we're going to say over and over again is this: the best promotion is a good book. Better promotion is more good books.

Let's take a look at another topic we have discussed on the Write It Forward blog.

AGENTS PUBLISHING AUTHORS IS ANOTHER MAJOR SHIFT IN PUBLISHING

Another shift in publishing is agents having to redefine their roles. Agents don't exist without the author. So the first question becomes: SHOULD Agents publish authors? Many are pointing out an inherent conflict of interest. If the agency is taking 15% either way — traditional publishing or self-publishing, we don't think they'd screw a client out of a traditional publishing deal to go with them. They'd steer the client to where they both saw the most money in the long run. However, there is also the possibility the agent could go for a deal where he/she made the most money, and that might not be in the author's overall best interest. Ultimately, though, an agent who starts publishing people is no longer an agent. Trying to be both is not only confusing, but it has many problems.

Most of the people screaming that this is 'bad,' 'a conflict of interest,' 'illegal,' 'they should all be taken out and shot,' have no dog in this hunt anyway, so why should they care? We think this is a case where each writer has to make their own decision. We've seen authors work with their agents, who have sold many books in New York, take their backlist and "assist" their clients in the self-publishing platform, and all parties involved are quite happy with the end result.

The problem is many new writers, or writers who don't have good agents, aren't very well educated on all the nuances, especially a new writer with no experience in publishing. Not only are many writers not educated, but many agents aren't educated in all that goes into making a digital reading experience. Caveat Emptor.

The thing that is most dangerous for many authors isn't just agents wanting to publish you, but agents and e-publishers who work under the theory of throwing many titles out there, each making a little bit of money, rather than focusing on a few titles, marketing the heck out of them, and making a lot of money off a few authors. Thus making the few authors a lot of money. Your average author via an ePublisher is earning less than one thousand dollars per title. Your average self-published author is in the same boat. Mark Coker at Smashwords freely admits they make their money off a lot of self-published books selling a few copies each, rather than a few authors selling a ton of copies. With that said, Mark Coker does a bang-up job of helping all authors by creating an environment that makes publishing relatively easy for authors. (We will discuss his "style guide" when we discuss formatting and file conversions.)

The reality is agencies are turning to this because they have to in order to generate income. Writers have to generate income, too. The question becomes: is it worth it to you to give a percentage to someone else to assist you in your digital/self-publishing endeavor?

Another thing these agents are going to discover is that they actually can't do all the work that is needed to produce and maintain an eBook for just 15%. There is a lot more involved in the process than they realize, as you'll see as you go through this material.

Still, an agency is not a publisher. Which brings us to:

The key question is not whether an agent *should* publish you, but rather *can* agents publish you? What makes an agent think they know something about ePublishing? First, they're not even print publishers. They're used to negotiating contracts, not publishing books. So while they can bring some of their experience in publishing to bear, they don't have experience as publishers. And even publishers don't have much experience in ePublishing since they are traditionally focused on print publishing and have a vested interest in keeping that focus.

Perhaps the question should be: who **CAN** publish you?

The issue is this: in a field agents have no experience in, what expertise does an agent bring to self-publishing an author that the author can't find elsewhere? We've been running Who Dares Wins Publishing for two years and we can tell you the learning curve to being an ePublisher is steep, brutal, and we both have two full-time jobs keeping it going.

Sure, these agents are delving into ePublishing, along with many other people in publishing. Most will probably hire someone to do the technical and other work for them, but that begs the question of why is the author giving up 15% to go through the agent who will hire the person the author could have hired on their own for a one-time fee? However, we don't believe publishing an eBook is a one-time deal that never has to be addressed again. It's a dynamic process that needs to be updated. It's the reason we are a team. Jen does most of the technical stuff and when we realize a change needs to be made, she is the one that goes into the files, makes the changes, and then reloads the eBooks. Paying her a percentage could be looked at in one of two ways: First, it keeps her invested in the success of all our books. If Bob were to pay her a flat, one-time fee for her services, her commitment to the success of his books would be different. More than that, there would be a fee every time Bob learned something new about eBooks and made the decision to adjust his digital books either by updating or using a new technique. Jen, however, was not an agent, nor does she act as one. Her experience is based in business and technology. The partnership makes sense based on our individual goals and the goals we set forth when we created Who Dares Wins Publishing.

Agents do bring experience in selling other rights, such as audio and foreign, but there are agents who are now focusing on working with successful self-published authors to do just that.

There is actually a good news/bad news to everything in publishing and with the way things are currently, it's hard to keep up with everything. While New York is slow to change, the rest of publishing is changing lightning fast. That seems like a contradiction in terms, but New York is reacting to the change in distribution while the rest of us are acting to the changes in the reader experience.

So how do you thrive in the chaos of the changing climate in publishing?

"Everything in war is very simple. But the simplest thing is difficult."
Karl Von Clausewitz

This was one of the lessons taught at West Point and re-affirmed during Bob's time in the Special Forces. He was trained to excel in chaos.

Bob was at the Pacific Northwest Writers Conference in Bellevue, WA, and listened to what people were saying, especially at the agent panel and then the editor panel and here's his summation:

Pretty much no one can clearly see the big picture of publishing from the writer to the reader. People are experts in their niches, but the overall concept is much murkier for most. Sort of the way the poor Infantryman in his foxhole has no clue how the overall battle is going, but he knows what the inside of his foxhole looks like. And many people in publishing are hunkering down in their foxholes.

We're thriving in the chaos of publishing. For Bob it feels like he's back on his A-Team. We're not hunkering down in our foxhole. We're acting instead of reacting and that's the future of publishing.

Earlier in this section we mentioned Sourcebooks and their recent announcement. The problem is they are a little behind the time. Forward thinkers will think beyond the current situation. Five years ago, they should have been looking at ways to solve the problem of making a digital book. It's not like they didn't exist.

A key aspect of branding (something we will talk about in section three) is what is known as "the creation story." How did something/someone come into existence? We hear names like Jeff Bezos or Steve Jobs; not only do we know the names and what companies they created, but we almost feel as though we personally know them because we know their "creation story." There is a creation story to digital books and how they came to be. What is your role in the digital age as an author?

SECTION TWO: PLAN FOR SUCCESS

If we don't know where we are going, we're likely to get lost. Before we can plan out our path, we have to know our options.

Bob Mayer and Jen Talty

TYPES OF PUBLISHING

The 21st century has brought with it many changes in technology and with those changes have come options. Every writer starts out in the same place. They have a passion to write and bring their stories to their readers. However, not every writer will take the exact same path to their readers.

There are many roads to Oz and even what each of us believes Oz to be varies from person to person.

There are no one size fits all publishing packages. Each writer must decide for themselves which option is the best for them. In order to do that, it is important to understand you do have options, but as you move toward your goals and achieve them, your options may shift. Having an open mind is one of the reasons we are successful at Who Dares Wins Publishing. Being able to see the big picture, as it fits into your personal plan will help you succeed. There are many pundits declaring their way is the *only* way to succeed in publishing, but anyone who claims that is naïve.

Our goal has been to break Bob out. One of the supporting goals was to publish his backlist. Another was to look at possible alternative and traditional publishing models for future books. Yes, traditional is still a viable option for any writer, depending on goals.

We've recently seen a lot of discussion regarding "indie" versus "traditional" and with that has come some name-calling. Bob was probably the first one to coin the term "hybrid" author, and, in reality, the overall best thing is to have as many different income streams as possible as a writer, including digital, print, audio, teaching, and whatever else your imagination can come up with.

We are going to lay out the basics of each type as we see them. You may have already chosen your path; however, read each one with an open mind.

Traditional Publishing

Three years from idea to bookstore, on average, although publishers are beginning to realize they have to be faster in a digital world.

Generally, it is writer finishing the book (1 year), submit to agent, submit to editor (1 year), if accepted the publisher produces the book (1 year) and the sales force then distributes it to bookstores where hopefully your book will get in the hands of the reader.

The author gets an advance, which 90% don't earn out (earn enough in royalties to equal the advance), and if they do, then the author gets royalties. Print is generally 6-10% of list price and eBooks are anywhere from 15% to 35% of list price. This is of course after your agent takes their 15%.

If you don't have the numbers on your profit and loss statement, the odds are the publisher doesn't renew you for more books, in essence firing you. 90% of first books fail.

The truth is, as bookstores go out of business, and the ones still standing order fewer books, the author's print run is drastically reduced, especially for the midlist author. Add that to a requirement for a higher sell-through rate, the chances of success are narrowing even more. The stores that do carry books such as Sam's Club, Wal-Mart, etc., stock only the best sellers.

Traditional publishing is not dead. It's evolving. There are valid reasons for writers to choose this path. It is just one of many. It could be the ultimate goal, or a supporting goal, but it is an option.

A big thing to consider is that print still sells a lot of books. The key is those numbers are skewed toward a handful of mega-bestselling authors.

ePublisher or non-traditional publisher

Small presses such as Ellora's Cave, The Wild Rose Press and others, take about a year or so from acceptance to release date.

They generally work on a no advance business model. In essence profit sharing, which we believe will seep into traditional publishing more and more. The author gets paid a higher royalty. Generally the royalty is about 35-40% of gross profit, or some might call it gross receipts or gross revenue. There are publishers that calculate royalties net receipts, and net isn't a good thing unless the publisher has very transparent books.

A lot of people don't really understand the difference between net and gross. Simply put, net is after expenses, gross is before. Some people believe that gross profit is a bad term. Perhaps gross revenue is a better one. The bottom line is you want to make sure that the publisher is paying royalties based on gross *everything*, before any expenses. For example, we pay our authors a 50% royalty. So, at Amazon, we get 70% (if priced between $2.99 and $9.99). If the eBook is priced at $2.99 and Amazon is paying us 70%, that means our gross profit is $2.09. The author gets 50% of the $2.09, which comes out to $1.05. None of our expenses are taken out of what we receive from Amazon. Most publishers calculate royalties based on cover price, which avoids this problem. If a publisher says they are paying royalties off of net, you have to find out what they consider legitimate expenses to deduct before paying your royalties, especially if you are going with a no advance, profit sharing model.

One of the perks of self-publishing is not sharing the piece of the pie. And many ePublishers don't promote other than slapping the book on the website and uploading it to the various platforms. This is why we cross promote our authors at Who Dares Wins Publishing and established *Readers Rule* — to cross promote and build readership.

The key thing to consider with an ePublisher is what services they offer you in return for their slice of the royalties. Consider the long term when doing this. For example, when Bob uses Audible's ACX program to do audio on his books, he has a choice: pay the audio talent a one time up front fee or go with a 50-50 split on royalties with the talent. He has chosen to go with the one-time up front fee, even though it means a substantial outlay of money, because he's in it for the long haul and figures the books will earn out that fee and then he'll receive 100% of the royalties.

Self-Publishing

The author controls when, where and how. The author takes on all the risk and all the expenses, but also gets all the profit. And there will be expenses: cover art editing, file conversions. etc.

Reality check. The odds of being successful in self-publishing are the same as in traditional publishing. Not only do you have to write good books, but you have to find ways to generate buzz and word of mouth. It's not easy. But, it is a viable option. Additionally, even if you are traditionally published, unless you get a large advance (close to seven figures), you're still going to have to do all these other promotional and marketing things to succeed anyway.

The key here is to look at self-publishing as a business and that it takes about 3-5 years to build a solid foundation for a business. We've been at this for 2 years and we're still building that solid base. It's the long tail. 95% of those self-publishing will quit, so one of the keys to success is perseverance.

When we published *The Jefferson Allegiance*, the first weekend it was released it rose to #2 on the Nook. We were selling thousands of just that title a day. It went on for a few weeks, but slowly started to drop. We remained in the top 100 for a month, but continued to falter, which is normal for 99% of all titles. In print publishing, *The Jefferson Allegiance* would now be considered dead and no longer racked. Not so with digital. We've moved on to the next part of our business plan. We're seeing it move up on other platforms and working on promotion for the long tail.

The long tail is also important when considering making writing the priority. The more titles you have available for sale, the greater the possibility for more income spread over a wider base.

Indies "vs." Tradionals: The elephant in the room

Authors have a choice in publishing. That's the good news. The bad news is, depending on how people view the choice, they appear to be taking sides and viewing one choice as "good and smart" and the opposite as "bad and dumb."

Adding to the conflict is the fact that others with a stake in the issue: booksellers, editors, agents, indie bookstores, aliens from Area 51, etc. are wading into it with their own opinions.

We're going to address some of the issues.

Established Authors

One of Bob's posts at Write It Forward showed how four of the major writing organizations wouldn't recognize a self-published writer. Yet on the PAN (Published Author Network) loop of RWA, most of it is now filled with posts about how to self-publish. We find that odd. What we're really seeing is a Hybrid Author. One who has a contract with a traditional publisher and also owns rights to some backlist, which they're self-publishing. This is a win-win for all involved. There is also a reverse to that: authors who have success self-publishing and then get picked up by traditional publishers. This is a growing trend.

In fact, it would behoove publishers who control rights, but aren't pushing them, to renegotiate with their authors. Give them a much higher royalty rate, or even more drastic, do reverse royalties. Give the rights back to the authors with a contract where they pay you a percentage of what they sell, say 25%. We guarantee you will make more money than you imagine if that author is making 75% self-publishing the titles and promoting them. Bob offered this deal to Random House for *Area 51* and was ignored. Then they just gave him the rights to all his books. We're selling tons of these books now. We sell more in one day in eBook than what they used to sell in six months. The reason for this is that no one cares more about a book and selling it than the author—but only if they are making money. This is another inherent problem with the advance system that is hardly ever discussed. In many instances, traditional authors have a disincentive to promote books that have never earned out—the desire to have the book's rights revert back to them with lackluster sales so they can then self-publish the title. If an author realizes they will never earn out on a title simply because the publisher has not printed enough copies and/or is not putting any push behind the eBooks at all, what motivation they do have to promote and market the book other than their own pride in their work?

New Authors

Write more. Too many people are pouring the time and energy into promotion that they should be putting into learning the craft of writing. The best promotion technique available is a good book. And more than one title. In fact, we think new authors should wait until they have at least three novels completed either in series or in single-title, before they focus a lot of their time on promoting.

Build Teams

Going it alone is very hard. Bob could have hired a contractor to do each individual cover, file conversions, etc. for the 50+ titles he has, but it made more sense for him to team up with Jen. Not only could she do great covers and make the eBooks, she revamped Bob's website, created a new website for Who Dares Wins Publishing, created our logs, manages all the blogs, made the Readers Rules Website...basically, Jen works full-time on the technical and marketing side of our business. Bob spends several hours a day on promotion. And our authors all cross promote each other. We think writers should band together, especially if they have books in the same genres.

Foreign markets

This is expanding daily. UK Kindle. Kindle Germany. France. Spain. And soon India. Even Barnes and Nobles is getting into the foreign markets. iBooks currently has over 32 stores across the globe.

The reality is eBooks will spread to more foreign markets as the platforms expand. We just uploaded *Bodyguard of Lies* in German and we are currently having *Area 51* and *Atlantis* translated into Spanish.

Agents, publishers and bookstores

Adapt to this new reality. The focus needs to shift from the traditional distribution end to the author and the book and, most important, selling to the reader.

Accept Hybrid Authors and support them

Bob's backlist selling 1,000 books a day is an excellent launching platform for new titles, but in twenty years, no publisher viewed his backlist as an asset. We never completely understood that, although distribution was a chokepoint, but now, with eBooks, someone like Bob is, frankly, gold. Yet, publishers have little interest, going about business as usual.

The three-headed Hydra of Publishing that's consuming itself

There are three main camps in publishing and they're not doing a very good job of communicating with each other. As Bob learned on his Special Forces A-Team, the key to a great team is for the leaders to insure that the specialists in their areas work with each other efficiently and positively so the team achieves its goal. It's not to insure that each specialist is the absolute best at their job, but rather that the TEAM is the best it can be. There is a subtle, but huge difference in this leadership philosophy that we don't see occurring in publishing

In the publishing business we have three main camps (and that's excluding readers, who are the body and soul of publishing):

The content providers. Called writers.

The business people: Called agents, editors, bookstores, etc.

The technical people: The people who transform what the writer produces into the new world of digital publishing. But here is where the lines start to blur. They're also the people who are advising the other two camps on how to use the digital world to market and promote and sell eBooks. Often, though, with little idea of what it takes to produce the product or how the business runs or how readers buy books.

For example, we've seen several articles lately where the topic was how the book as we know it is dead, that Amazon will hire hundreds of monkeys to lock in warehouses to produce books and there's no place for writers any more. After all, anyone can write a novel, correct? Wrong.

We submit that a huge misconception in publishing right now is a lack of understanding of what it really takes to produce a good book. After all, if you've never written one, how could you? Not only that, but writers, other than the big brand names, have always been treated as replaceable parts. Just look at the slush pile. All those people desperate to be content providers. Except for two things: it's called the slush pile for a reason; and, not many content providers (i.e. authors), really understand what's going on in the business and technical sides of publishing.

An Introduction to Self-Publishing

Self-publishing is not the easy route. It's not a get rich fast route. It's not the "if I can't do New York then I'll self-publish route" and it's not the "go to crap plan." Self-publishing in today's world of digital books is a business plan. As we said before, just because you CAN self-publish, doesn't mean you should. The decision to self-publish must be a vehicle to help you achieve your main strategic goal as a writer.

Today, Jen spent a good portion of her day loading eBooks to Kobo, talking with an SEO specialist and finally wrapping up with a conference call with a Public Relations person who is putting us in contact with an Entertainment PR person who has media ideas for Bob Mayer. For the most part, an author doesn't need a PR person, however, an opportunity has come up (through networking at conferences) where we might be able to get Bob in front of some audiences that influence book buyers, in a big way. Meanwhile, Bob was busy making edits to the final *Area 51* book, which will be loaded shortly. He also put out a fire regarding a potential cover issue (we will discuss more in depth when we get to that section). Not to mention he did a few interviews.

That's just one work day.

All of this is why we have chosen to build our team.

Self-publishing is a lot easier than it used to be, and more and more people are doing it. The actual click on the publishing button doesn't take but a "click."

What is hard about self-publishing is what is hard about traditional publishing, and that is making a living at it. What is hard is getting the attention of the people who are sitting in decision-making seats, like who gets featured on the homepage at Nook, and who doesn't. What is hard is figuring out specific keywords (when you only get seven) that best fit you and your book,e and will get you the most hits on Amazon when potential customers do a search. This is critical because how many people actually know to search for YOU or the title of your book?

In self-publishing you are in complete control and you are responsible for your success or failure. There are no bad cover artists to blame. No horrible editors that didn't understand. No publishing house that refused to put their marketing money behind you. It's you, and you alone who are responsible for your success and the promise you make to your readers.

Bob posted a blog at Write It Forward about the fighting and name calling between those who traditionally publish and those who self-publish. It's gotten out of hand in some cases. No matter the path, we have to remember that publishing is a business. If you go with New York you are part of their business path, if you do it yourself, it is your business path. There is good and bad in both options. One must decide for themselves what they can do, what they will do, what they can't do and what they won't do in order to make the best decision.

When we first started Who Dares Wins Publishing, there seemed to be two camps in publishing. New York is the only way to go. OR. Screw New York, it's dead. What we're seeing now is that while there are still two camps amongst authors, the lines have started to blur. This is because eBooks are a reality and publishers are getting with the program.

Both camps are right. Digital is a reality and more and more people are using reading devices. Publishers do need to make some major adjustments. Dorchester is proof of that. Traditional distribution doesn't work. The traditional way of publishing is beyond flawed. New York is producing eBooks. They do acknowledge the need to embrace the digital age.

Can any writer self-publish?

The answer is a big, fat YES. Technology has made this a relatively simple process. We say relatively because there is a steep learning curve and even after you've "learned" the basics, if you want to do it right and maximize your efforts in order to increase your sales, you're going to have to invest a lot of time and effort. It's not a get rich quick scheme, but you can turn a pretty profit.

There are a lot of options out there for the author who wants to self-publish. You can use a vanity press (we don't recommend that route). You can go with something like Smashwords and let them be your publisher and distributor to various eBookstores. LuLu is another option for both eBooks and POD. You can just publish on Amazon's KDP (Kindle Direct Publishing). Or Barnes and Noble's PubIt. Both Amazon and PubIt have made the process pretty painless. We're going to talk about some of these shortly.

But this brings us to the element of time again. Yes, anyone can self-publish. But in order to be successful, you have to invest a huge amount of time and energy into finding what will be the best option for you. It is not one-size fits all. What works for one, might not work for another. And, all we've discussed so far is getting your book ready for publication. And just the book. Not the cover, etc. But the bottom line is, anyone who puts their mind to it, can self-publish their book.

Should anyone self-publishing their book?

The answer to this question is a big fat DEPENDS. Why? When we first started with Who Dares Wins Publishing, we believed the most successful self-published authors came from two backgrounds.

The first being previously published authors with backlist. The second would be a non-fiction author with a platform.

However, we used to believe that if you don't fit into those two categories you might as well pack up and go home. That isn't necessarily the case anymore. The key is content, which is King. Do you have quality content? Is your material, whether it be fiction or non-fiction well written, edited and something readers want? The other key is promotion, which is Queen. They rule together. If you plan on simply putting your stuff out there and think the readers are just going to flock to you, your odds of success are rather low. You have to be willing to promote, and promote hard.

Pay The Writer

What value do you put on your time as a writer? It's not just a question about the pricing of an eBook (which we will discuss) but a question of valuing and respecting our profession.

Many writers don't value themselves and therefore they have taught those around them not to value or respect the need to hone the craft of writing. Too often, writing is the last thing writers put down as their priority. In order to be successful in any profession, one has to see the value in the profession and put in the time necessary to achieve desired goals.

You cannot complete a novel if you don't start a novel. You can't start the novel if you don't carve out the space and time needed to write the novel. If you look back to the three areas and the 9 tools Bob diagrams in *Write It Forward: From Writer to Successful Author* under the first area WINS is the tool WHERE. Where are you going to write your bestselling novel? Where are you going to promote your bestselling novel? If you have not established the where, there is no time like the present to carve out that space. Whether it is a closet in the basement, or the dining room table, it doesn't matter. It is your space. When Susan Wiggs was a full-time teacher, mother and house-wife, she told her family that from nine to midnight was her writing time. Her family respected that, and more importantly, Susan committed to it. She's now a #1 *NY Times* Bestselling Author.

Under the area WHO, we have the tools CHANGE and COURAGE. Courage comes into play by making the Change. If you are not where you want to be with your writing or your career as an author, you must change what you are doing. This is linked to the area

DARES and the tools COMMAND and COMMUNICATE. We must communicate to those around us that is our time. And, very important, remember you are in control of your writing career, more so now than ever before.

There is more to *pay the writer* than valuing our time and profession.

We recently followed a discussion about what writers should charge when they're invited to speak. Many of those responding posted about how they didn't charge anything, or only expenses, etc. Very few posted that they charged what they felt their time was worth. In fact, it seemed as if most felt grateful that they were invited in the first place.

Being the troublemaker Bob is, he posted a link to Harlan Ellison's YouTube video reference *Pay The Writer* (http://youtu.be/mj5IV23g-fE).

Write It Forward is about author advocacy. An indie bookstore closes, there's an article in the paper, a blurb in PW, people lament, but an indie writer goes out of business there's not a blip on the radar. We've found taking this position is not publicly popular. On Twitter, on loops, on Facebook, on the Write It Forward Blog, there are people who have attacked Bob for putting the author first. The funny thing is, though, Bob then got a ton of emails and DMs privately, telling him they appreciate what he's doing.

We don't like talking about money in America. In "White Palace," Susan Sarandon's character asks her yuppie boyfriend how much he makes. He doesn't want to tell, and her response is basically: we can have sex, but you can't tell me how much you make? Apparently not.

Before we get crucified, yes, we do think one should volunteer to help certain non-profits. But also remember, a lot of people working at non-profits are getting paid and often they earmark funds for speakers. Schools, for example, often set aside funds for speakers and there's nothing wrong with accepting payment, as this broadens your revenue base, a key to having a career as a writer. We also donate time, money and books. At Who Dares Wins Publishing we donate a percentage of our gross revenue at the end of each year to the *Special Operations Warrior Foundation* (http://www.specialops.org/). We've given made numerous talks and presentations gratis over the years. However, there is a difference between giving back to your community (doing select free workshops, etc.) and being asked to forgo your ability to earn a living.

We teach people how to treat us. This is a tenet of Write It Forward. When Bob branched out from the writing world into other businesses with his **Who Dares Wins** (http://bobmayer.org/WDW_Business.html) consulting, he was surprised to find that if he quoted a speaking/consulting fee that was too low, he was treated as if what he was presenting was not very worthwhile. Many business consultants, life coaches, motivational speakers and other corporate trainers have no problem asking to be paid for their expertise. Writers need to consider themselves professionals.

You have to consider not only the actual talk, but your expertise. When Bob presents Who Dares Wins, he's not just giving a company a two-hour presentation. He's giving them the benefit of decades of experience as a Special Forces student, team leader, operations officer, commander, soldier, instructor at the JFK Special Warfare Center and consultant to previous organizations. Also, being a *NY Times* bestselling author who has sold millions of books and started up a successful publishing company. That stuff was hard to come by. It's worth something.

We do feel uncomfortable when someone asks how much we charge for a talk, particularly in the writing world, when we know money is tight for the organizations. Bob remembers, though, what he was told one year at the Maui Writers Conference. A CEO of a very successful company told him that in the corporate world, to get the kind of high level expertise that was being given at Maui (Terry Brooks, Elizabeth George, John Saul, Dorothy Allison, Robin Cook, Frank McCourt, Dan Millman, etc. etc.) one would expect to pay tens of thousands of dollars. And all these best-selling authors were getting was a plane ticket and a hotel room for their collective experiences and expertise.

We believe writers should value their expertise. If asked what you charge, consider who is asking, what is being asked, and what value it will have to those who receive your expertise. Remember, all they can do is say no, or tell you what they can pay. And you can always negotiate. One technique we use for some of our day-long presentations is give a percentage of our book sales at the event back to the organization. This is a win-win situation.

Publishing is changing. Writers used to be treated (except for the few brand name authors) as the bottom rung of the food chain. We were interchangeable parts. We're not any more. All those people between us and our readers (agents, editors, publishers, book reps, bookstores) are the ones whose jobs are in danger. The ones who are adapting will prosper, just as writers who do will. If we don't respect ourselves, we're not going to get respect from others.

Another problem writers run into is the business model of traditional publishing. Advances are shrinking and it's very hard for a writer to make a living. Many writers just want to be published so they'll take any deal that's offered. Remember, no deal is better than a bad deal. No agent is better than a bad agent. The one true power writers have is the ability to say *no*, yet few exercise it. That's fine, but it's important to go back and take a look at your strategic goal and make sure whatever deal or path you choose to take is the right one for you.

Who Dares Wins: The Green Beret Way to Conquer Fear and Succeed by Bob Mayer, was published by Pocket Books a division of Simon & Schuster, Inc. in June of 2009. Who Dares Wins is the motto of the British Special Air Service and has been used by nine elite special-forces units across the world. The words, Who Dares Wins, sum up the way Bob views the world and is the foundation for his success.

In ***Who Dares Wins: The Green Beret Way to Conquer Fear and Succeed***, Bob takes three Areas (Who, Dares, Wins) and breaks them down into nine specific tools.

Area One: Wins
　　Tools: What, Why and Where
Area Two: Who
　　Tools: Character, Change and Courage
Area Three: Dares
　　Tools: Communicate, Command and Complete

These make up what Bob refers to as the *Circle of Success*.

Bob has taken this unique concept from his world as a Green Beret to the world of writing. He then brought it to an area sorely lacking in publishing with *Write It Forward: From Writer to Successful Author.*

The Circle of Success not only helps individuals improve the quality of their lives and careers, but is the foundation to courage, which leads to success in the changing world of publishing.

The circle of success is all about figuring out what you want, planning out how to get it, overcoming the obstacles that stand in your way and communicating your plan to the world. It is about taking command and control of your career and your life and making it all that you dreamed it could be. No one plans to fail, but when you don⬚ factor in all the possibilities and look at all the possible roads to Oz, you are limiting yourself.

Adapt or Die.

It sounds harsh, and it is. But in order to succeed in the current publishing environment, authors must change the way they think and do business. Authors must change. This section is dedicated to helping authors define what it is they want so they can make best possible decisions and be the author their readers will connect to.

WRITE IT FORWARD AND DEFINING GOALS

"I'm convinced fear is at the root of most bad writing."
Stephen King

In everything that we teach, whether it be novel writing, Write It Forward, or digital publishing, we always start with goals. It is important that you state your one strategic goal as a writer because if you don't know where you are going, you are likely to get lost. If you don't have supporting goals that support your strategic goal, you will never achieve it. For example, if you don't know your strategic writing goal, you can't come up with an efficient and focused plan for attending a writing conference and as a result, you will be wasting both your time and money. We cover that in our *Writers Conference Guide: Getting The Most Out of Your Time and Money*.

Just as it is important to know what you want in your novel, it is key to know what you want from your career. Whether it is becoming a *NY Times* Bestseller, or to quote Parnell Hall "I want to be the king of Kindle," your efforts must support that.

Every couple of months Bob sends Jen an email that states something along the lines of: *by the end of the year I want to sell X # of books, make X # of dollars, have ABC manuscript at Encore, have the attention of XYZ at B&N and have new work done.* Or perhaps it is Jen sending Bob the email that states: *by the end of the year I want this part of the marketing campaign in place, this part of the branding/creation story written, and have the survival guide completed for you to go through and have a draft of my new fiction work done.*

All of those are supporting goals to the main goal of breaking Bob Mayer out as a household name in the world of fiction. Everything we do supports that goal. We revisit that goal often. We *plan* and then *execute* based on that ONE SPECIFIC goal.

We mentioned in the first section the idea of the creation story and Jeff Bezos of Amazon. He sat in the back of his car as his wife drove while he wrote his plan for Amazon. Our plan began over a cup of coffee at a conference and then in a long- running email conversation about what we wanted and how we planned on getting there.

What is your goal? And how will execute a plan to achieve that goal?

You can "pants" your way through your novel, but you can't "pants" your way to success.

As you read this section think about these four key questions:

- What do I want to achieve with my writing career?
- What publishing path, or variety of paths, will help me achieve that goal?
- What else do I need to be doing in order to achieve my goal?
- What is preventing me from achieving my goal?

It is crucial to your career that you can clearly define your path. Success only happens if you define what success really means for you.

We are actually going through this process again right now as we go into a new year. It can be harder than you think to make your goals concrete. We suggest getting out pen and paper, or keyboard, and writing down your thoughts down as we go through it.

What is Write It Forward

Write It Forward focuses on educating writers how to be successful authors and helping them conquer their fears. Many writers become too focused on either the writing or the business end. Write It Forward integrates the two, putting the control back into the author's hands.

Authors learn by trial and error and networking with other authors. Sometimes it's the blind leading the blind. When this happens, writers are often given poor advice. It is well-meaning advice, but not always accurate and generally tainted by point-of-view.

Given the drastic changes the industry is currently undergoing, the most knowledgeable people admit they have little idea where the industry will be in a year. However, one thing remains constant: writers produce the product and readers consume the product.

Agents, editors, publishers, and bookstores are currently the primary contractors, processors, and sellers of that product. On-line retailers also offer an option that didn't exist just a few years ago. While most agents and editors normally get educated in a career path starting at the bottom of an agency/publishing house, writers, from the moment they sign a contract or self-publish their book, are thrust immediately into the role of author as well as promoter. For the new author it's sink or swim. Unfortunately, with the lack of author training, most sink. First novels in traditional publishing have a 90% failure rate, which is simply foolhardy. First novels that are self-published have an even higher failure rate because they lack even the help a traditional agent and publisher gives. We submit that the overall success rate for self-publishing is the same as the success rate for getting an agent, publisher, etc. and breaking out.

The learning curve to becoming a successful author is a steep one. In the past, the author might have had years to learn, and when needed, re-invent one's self, but the business is now moving at a much faster pace. It's expected that authors not only have to write the books, but also become promoters of their books. Interestingly enough, Promoter (ESTP) is the complete opposite of Author (INFJ) in the Myer-Briggs personality indicator. It's difficult to go from one mindset to the other. Not only do you have to be Author and Promoter, you must also be Seller (ESJF).

Let's take a look at some exercises we pose in Write It Forward that can help you succeed as a digital author:

What is your strategic goal as a writer? Where do you want to be in three to five years? Answer this succinctly in one sentence, giving an external yardstick by which to measure whether you've achieved this goal or not, and also a time-lock for achieving this goal. An example would be:

"In three years, I want to be selling enough eBooks per month to earn $8,000 before taxes."

While this might seem a cold and calculating goal, the reality is this allows you to clearly determine your subordinate, tactical goals. If you're pricing eBooks at $2.99, you know exactly how many you have to sell per month to earn $8k. Which might make you consider pricing at $3.99 and selling fewer copies. Or pricing at .99 and selling a lot more copies.

Once you figure out this goal, you should know your Why for the goal. In fact, your Why might determine your What. The aforementioned goal comes out of a Why: I can make a living as a writer earning $8,000 a month. In essence, it would seem your goal is to make a living as a writer. But for a strategic goal, you have to be very specific with an external measuring stick and a time lock. Anything vaguer, and you will easily get lost.

I'll do anything to succeed as a writer, except don't ask me to do....?

Whatever completes that sentence is your greatest fear as a writer. This question is a great way of finding the one fear that is crippling you. *We must attack the ambush.*

Your patrol is walking along a trail and suddenly you are fired upon from the right. Your fear wants you to jump in the convenient ditch to the left — to avoid the ambush.

However, if the ambush is set up correctly — that ditch is mined and you'll die if you dive in. In life, avoiding problems by running from them doesn't solve the problem.

Your next fear-driven instinct is to just hit the ground. Stay where you are and do nothing. Except you're in the kill zone and if you stay there, well, you'll get killed. We all want to ignore problems. Because that's the inherent nature of a problem. But ignoring your greatest problem will keep you in the kill zone and the result is inevitable.

The third thing you want to do is run forward or back on the trail to get out of the kill zone--escape. Except, if the ambush is executed properly, the heaviest weapons are firing on either end of the kill zone. And you'll die. We want to avoid problems by going back to the past or imagining it will get better in the future even if we don't change anything.

The correct solution is the hardest choice because it requires courage: you must conquer your fear, turn right and assault the ambushing force. It is the best way to not only survive, but win. To tackle problems, you must face them.

In the Write It Forward program, we focus on developing authors. Most writing programs focus on the writing, but I believe it's important to focus on the person producing the writing. And, as Stephen King says: "I believe fear is at the root of most bad writing."

Here's a question every writer has to answer: "I'll do whatever it takes to succeed except don't ask me to do FILL IN THE BLANK."

Whatever that one thing is, it is the one thing you *must* do to succeed.

Write what you know — maybe write what you are afraid to know. I see many writers who avoid writing what they should be writing because it would mean confronting their fears. Be curious about your fear — it's a cave, but instead of a monster inside, you could find treasure.

Remember, fear is an emotion. Action can occur even when your emotions are fighting it. Taking action is the key to conquering fear. Attacking the ambush.

How do you expand your comfort zone by venturing into your courage zone?

Every day try to do something that you dislike doing, but need to do.

If you're introverted, talk to a stranger every day.

If you're a practical person, do something intuitive every day.

Do the opposite of your Myers-Briggs character.

So what is the thing that you truly don't want to do, but need to in order to succeed as a writer?

How high is your 'imposter syndrome' as a writer? This is a key area in Write It Forward. It really comes into play as a digital author, because for most of us, we are taken out of our comfort zone both by the technology and the need to promote. Also, if you are self-publishing, you don't have the validation of having gone through an agent and gotten a book contract.

The imposter syndrome is when you have difficulty internalizing your accomplishments. All those things you've achieved: completing the book, publishing it, sales, promotions, publication, best-seller lists, etc. are thrown out. Instead, people look to external things like luck and contacts that had little to do with their own efforts as the reason for the successes they've achieved. Inside themselves, many people feel like they are *fooling* everyone. What's particularly hard about that is the more success a person achieves, the greater the fear of being found out as a fraud becomes.

A big problem with the imposter syndrome for the self-published author is that you start relying more on chance and luck than on your hard work, which can cause you to give up on the consistency needed for success.

Some ways to gauge how much of The Imposter Syndrome you have: The more you agree with the following statements, the higher your IS:

I can give the impression I am more competent than I really am

I often compare myself to those around me and consider them more intelligent than I am

I get discouraged if I'm not the 'best' in an endeavor

I hate being evaluated by others

49

If someone gives me praise for something I've accomplished, it makes me fear that I won't live up to his or her expectations in the future

I've achieved my current position via luck and/or being in the right place at the right time

When I think back to the past, incidents where I made mistakes or failed come more readily to mind than times when I was successful

When I finish a manuscript, I usually feel like I could have done so much better

When someone compliments me, I feel uncomfortable

I'm afraid others will find out my lack of knowledge/expertise

When I start a new manuscript, I'm afraid I won't be able to finish it, even though I've already finished X number of manuscripts

If I've been successful at something, I often doubt I can do it again successfully

If my agent tells me I'm going to get an offer on a book, I don't tell anyone until the contract is actually in hand

Women tend to agree more with IS statements than men. They also tend to believe that intelligence is a fixed trait that cannot be improved over time. Women who feel like imposters tend to seek favorable comparisons with their peers. Men who feel like imposters tend to avoid comparisons with their peers. Often, they work harder, even in the wrong direction, so other people won't think them incapable or dumb.

Overall, people who feel like imposters are constantly comparing their success against the achievements of others rather than viewing what they do as an end in itself. For writers, this can be very dangerous, because there will always be someone who is *doing it better* or *is more successful*. This is especially true in digital publishing where you can constantly check sales numbers. Also, on places like Kindleboards and industry blogs, you will see reports of people having great successes.

One thing to remember is that some of those posts aren't exactly the truth. The reality is that there are people inflating their numbers and their successes. We have seen cases where information reported is flat out false, or at least a misrepresentation of reality.

A technique to fight feeling like a fraud is to use a version of my HALO concept on yourself. Start from way outside yourself, diving in until you can see things clearly. Step outside and view things as if you are a stranger to yourself.

Examine your resume. Look at what you've accomplished in life. Ask yourself what kind of person would have achieved these things? Could a fraud have done this? When I query a conference to teach or apply to lead workshops or do keynotes, I have to send my bio. Sometimes I stop and read it and ask myself: what would I think of this person if I didn't know them, but just read this?

Focus on positive feedback. However, don't ignore negative feedback. The key is not to let the negative overwhelm you. While I look at Amazon reviews and rankings for business reasons, I don't focus on them emotionally. First, you have to realize that only a certain segment of the population posts reviews on Amazon. It's not a true sample of the population. Also, the motives for posting reviews often have nothing to do with your book.

Another interesting angle to feeling like a fraud is a study that showed when people with high Imposter Syndrome scores were asked to predict how they would do on an upcoming test, they tended to predict they would do poorly when around others. However, privately, they predicted they would do as well as those who had low Imposter Syndrome scores. What this means is some people adopt self-deprecation as a social strategy and are actually more confident than they let on. They lower other people's expectations and also appear humble. I believe, though, that doing so, can also subconsciously lower your own expectations and become a self-fulfilling prophecy.

On the flip side of feeling like a fraud, some people tend to overrate their abilities. A self-serving delusion is almost necessary in this world to just get out of bed in the morning at times. But take it too far and it can destroy you.

The bottom line on dealing with 'feeling like a fraud' is to internalize more of your accomplishments. I have all my published books in my office on the top of bookcases, all lined up. The row is over three feet wide. I look at it sometimes to fight the feeling that I can't write another book, that I can't get published again.

You have to believe in yourself. If you're unpublished, walk into the bookstores and don't let all those published authors overwhelm you. Use them to motivate you. Tell yourself you belong there. I always look and say, "Hey, these people got published, why can't I? I've never even heard of 90% of these people."

List your accomplishments. They can range from a picture of your family, degrees achieved, awards won, whatever. Put them where you write. Use them to remind yourself that you are not a fraud. *YOU ARE REAL.*

Are you in command of your writing career or are you counting on an agent or editor or just blind luck?

Do you know where you stand on the three P's: Platform, product and promotion?

Don't Let Fear Take You Down

As a former Infantryman and Green Beret, Bob learned a lot about fear. Now he's seeing it consuming publishing and authors. Too many people really believe it's better not to know reality rather than face the fact that perhaps they are approaching reality the wrong way. Letting go of the traditional world of publishing is tough. Bob knows. Been there. Done that.

Bookselling HAS changed and the amount of disinformation people in publishing are disseminating in a desperate attempt to save their jobs is staggering. Let's face it, eBooks are a game changer whether we jump on the digital wave or not.

Frankly, we think few in New York Publishing really understand the big picture of eBook publishing from writer to reader. They can see parts of it, but are usually limited by their own role in the business and by their owns wants and needs. We keep seeing panels at conferences made up of "experts" on digital publishing, but rarely are these people making their living off selling their own books through digital publishing, so we submit they are observers, not experts. That doesn't mean their opinion isn't valid, it just means it isn't the same as yours: the Digital Author. Bob had an editor from Random House tell him they were chasing the technology to see where it would lead — such a statement staggers the mind as the primary rule of combat is to act, not react.

Here's the thing we want authors to understand. Take your emotions out of it. Let go of your fear. You now have an opportunity that's unprecedented. You can reach your readers directly. You don't need all the middlemen. Learn from what we have accomplished, and others like us. From the authors doing it. Not the people theorizing about it. However, on the flip side, you can't do it all alone. You need to work with people who are experienced in the new technology and the new market for books. You can stay with the known or venture into the unknown where the future lies. You can keep switching deckchairs on the Titanic or you can find a ship that's actually going somewhere.

In all frankness, Bob wasn't thrilled with the prospect of self-publishing when Jen first started discussing the option back in 2009. Part of his hesitance was that he was uncertain about the viability of self-publishing and the eBook market. Bob knew the chances of success, and because his goal at the time was to "break out," he didn't think that would happen via self-publishing. That said, publishing his backlist was an entirely different story. His goals and our goals as a company have not really changed. What has changed is our mindset and the way we align our supporting goals. Everything we do is set up to help push us to the next level which will ultimately push us to our main strategic goal.

DEFINE YOUR GOALS

Now, we are going to repeat a couple of important questions. *What is my strategic goal as a writer? Where do I want to be in three to five years?*

We do want you to take the time to write this down. Then, write down some of your supporting goals that will help you achieve the main one. For example:

Main Strategic Goal: Be consistently earning $100,000 a month in 3 years
Supporting goals include:

- publish backlist, promote, get on top lists
- continue to consistently earn $50,000 a month in year one, $75,000 a month in year two.
- continue to publish front list and submit front list to key publishers with our plan
- gain the attention of those who make decisions in publishing
- create author buzz via social media and print
- sell foreign rights
- invest 33% of earnings back into the company in terms of promotion, marketing, convention and conference attendance, advertising, editing, audio, and foreign translations
- develop a strategy for "primal branding" and put it in place
- become an expert consultant in gaming and developing games with Bob Mayer series in mind

- produce 6 new titles per year by Bob
- attract at least 2 new authors per year
- increase advertising and promotion for all authors via Facebook, Google and other social media
- and many others

Now, each of these supporting goals needs specific plans. We are going to get into some of those specific plans.

Take a short break from reading and write down your STRATEGIC goal and all your SUPPORTING goals. Revisit these goals often. Put them where you can see them every single day. Whenever you are doing something related to your writing career, look at your goal and ask yourself, *is what I'm doing right now helping me achieve my goals?* By doing this, you will be able to remain focused.

THE THREE Ps: PLATFORM, PRODUCT, PROMOTION

By closely monitoring the publishing business, we see many different paths and approaches suggested to aspiring authors regarding everything from writing the book to publishing the book to promoting and building platform and brand. It's a very confusing time for publishing in general and many authors are finding themselves caught in the crossfire.

There's a lot of advice out there, much of it contradictory. We are going to sort this out for you with a template you can use to continue your own career path.

There's a simple reason for all the conflicting advice: no two authors are exactly the same. We all approach our careers with different goals. How we define those goals plays a key role in the questions we need to ask ourselves up front. Do I want traditional publishing? Is self-publishing a viable option for me? What other options are there? Or should I pack up and go home? Making an educated decision on our publishing path leads the author into this mass confusion of varying opinions on the subject. In an effort to bring some clarity to the issue, we offer up three variables and examine how they affect the way a writer should view getting published and, more important, their writing career.

The variables are:

Platform
Product
Promotion

Platform

Name recognition is what people think of, but there's more to platform than that. Are you an expert in your field? Do you have a special background that makes you unique? Everyone has some sort of platform, even if it's just your emotions, exemplified by Johnny Cash in *Walk The Line*, mining his anger into art. Bob uses the film clip of his audition at the beginning of his Write It Forward workshop, book and presentation, and shows how quickly Cash changed, mined his 'platform,' and was on his way to becoming a star. All within three minutes.

So the question you must ask yourself is: what is your platform?

Quote from Legally Blonde:

Professor Callahan (talking about Elle Woods): "Do you think she woke up one morning and said: *I think I'll go to law school today.*"

How did Elle Woods get in? She used her life experiences. The entrance video she made is really marketing brilliance when it comes to platform building.

When Jen was a young, starving college student, she worked as a receptionist for an outpatient rehabilitation facility. One day her boss came to her and said, "Jen, would you like more hours?" Of course she did. She needed money. "We want you to re-write our job description manual and our policy and procedural manuals."

This was her first taste of technical and creative writing rolled into one. The first thing she did was give everyone new job titles. She went from Receptionist to "Client Coordinator." The Billing Clerk became "Insurance Specialist" and the Outpatient Secretary became the "Patient Liaison." Her boss actually loved the titles, but did tell her she had a special talent for BS. Kind of fitting that her degree ended up being a B.S. in Business Education with a concentration in Marketing and Sales.

Platform is the amalgamation of who you are and your life experiences that you bring to any given table. Your platform grows and changes as you grow and change based on the choices you make.

Author Platform, or any platform for that matter, is what your life experiences have taught you. Elle may have just one day decided to go to law school, but becoming an expert at law took time and education and passion. How you choose to incorporate your education and life experiences into your overall plan is entirely up to you.

Don't get close-minded on platform. Traditional publishers immediately are looking at name recognition (brand) and ability to reach a market (which ties into promoting). They are going to focus on the top 10%. They aren't going to take many risks. Amanda Hocking was not a risk for St. Martins Press. She's had a well documented rise to the top of self-publishing. Amazon did not take a risk on Barry Eisler. They both had numbers and a strong platform to back it all up.

Remember that Platform and Brand are two different things, but connected very intimately. We will be doing an entire chapter on branding, but the basic difference is Platform is who you are, what you bring to the table, why you are an expert, and Brand is the feeling of who you are that translates to the customer.

You are part of the package deal when it comes to your books. Grow and develop your platform and your brand. Be open. Understand agents and publishers are watching. More important, so are your readers. They are who we need to reach.

Product

The book. Yes, you need a book. Or a proposal for a book. This is your content. Most authors become totally fixated on content, while ignoring platform and promotion. Do so at your peril.

Product is two fold in indie publishing. First are the words on the page. In a previous chapter we talked about the *Novel Writer's Toolkit* that we updated this year. Part of having a great product is taking the necessary steps in making it the best that it can be. In a later section we will discuss editing in greater detail, but make no mistake, your story must be better than the rest, and you must pay for good editing.

The second part of the product is the digital book and, in some cases, the print book. You can have the best-written book ever, but if the eBook has a dozen or so blank pages, or double indents, or any other digital mistakes, it will frustrate the reader. We will discuss the making of digital eBooks in a later chapter. You also need an eye-catching cover with a product description that is inviting to the reader.

Promotion

The ability to promote your book in various outlets is crucial. Can you develop a unique hook or angle that will get you media attention?

It's important to understand that promotion is a marketing tool. We're going to discuss Marketing as a whole soon, but in order to understand the three P's and where you fit as an author, your ability to promote (get the word out there) is essential, but it is only one part of your entire marketing package. Promotion is inside of marketing. It is one of the four elements in the marketing mix.

There is an argument that Marketing can potentially negate the need for sales. It's the idea that once great marketing and solid promotion are set in place it will bring more people "through the door" rather than having to go out and find your readers.

Another thing to consider in promotion are things like SEO (Search Engine Optimization). Setting metatags can help search engines find you, but if you don't know the HTML for metatags and how to use them, it will be harder for the SEOs to find you.

Also, you should understand analytics. Do you track hits to your website? Where do they come from? Where are people clicking out to? What key words are people using to find you? All these things fall under Marketing, but help you in promotional efforts. For example, we've done a few Facebook and Google ads and found that few people ever search for Thomas Jefferson, so using that as a keyword for *The Jefferson Allegiance* is not a good choice.

Just like Platform and Brand, Marketing and Promotion are a little different. Marketing is the plan, and Promotion is one part of the plan. One of the things we do on the Write It Forward blog is track where the hits are coming from and where people click to. We found something interesting about Facebook and Twitter. More than triple the number of people click to our website from Twitter than from Facebook. What does it mean? That Twitter is more of a *call to action* than Facebook. A *call to action* means when people land on your tweet or anywhere on your website or blog, they have to act by clicking on something or doing something that you want them to. When you send a tweet with a link to your website or blog, that is a *call to action*.

Having a Call to Action is huge in promotion. We're getting ready to send out a newsletter and in the newsletter there will be a call to action. If you buy something from the website, you will get a discount. In the newsletter analytics, we will look at the call to action and see how many clicks go to the website. We can also see if the promotion is effective.

If you consider these three variables, with a sliding scale from 'none' to 'the best,' you end up with an infinite variety of authors. To simplify matters, let's go with 'weak' and 'strong.' This gets us down to eight possible types of writers:

Strong Platform	Strong Product	Strong Promotion
Strong Platform	Strong Product	Weak Promotion
Strong Platform	Weak Product	Strong Promotion
Strong Platform	Weak Product	Weak Promotion
Weak Platform	Strong Product	Strong Promotion
Weak Platform	Strong Product	Weak Promotion
Weak Platform	Weak Product	Strong Promotion
Weak Platform	Weak Product	Weak Promotion

If you're in the latter line, fughhedaboutit as we used to say in the Bronx.

But for all the other combinations of the three P's, we can see a type of writer. Where do you fall? Where do you fall and where do you want to be?

These are no discrete entities. They all rely on each other. You have to consider that promotion is based on platform and product.

Product is often based on the platform. If you have a platform you will most likely write a book mining that platform (if you don't, well, perhaps reconsider?).

There's a degree of luck involved in promotion. In going viral. But luck goes to the person who climbs the mountain to wave the lightning rod about. It's called hard work. One key lesson we've learned at Who Dares Wins Publishing is consistency and repetition of message is key. Slack off for a week, and fughhedaboutit.

Product is the one thing you can improve the most by working on your craft. Go to conferences and take workshops or master classes from the greats. Low-Country RWA offers a beach retreat and a week-long master class. They bring in various successful authors who teach workshops on craft and on business. The atmosphere alone fosters creativity, and in the evening hours they run critique sessions. Bob is gearing up to run his *Write In The Woods (http://bobmayer.org)* series of intimate workshops for writers in Chapel Hill. For a full listing of conferences and workshops you can check out Shawguides (http://shawguides.com).

Online courses are quickly becoming a great way to work with authors and other experts at a lower cost. Don't limit yourself. If you write crime fiction, consider authors like Lee Lofland. He's got a great blog called *The Graveyard Shift* (leelofland.com/wordpress). We offer a variety of online workshops at *Write It Forward* (https://whodareswinspublishing.com/WIF_Workshops.html) on craft and we are expanding each year, bringing on other authors and experts.

If you are not a natural born promoter or have a unique background, these two areas might be a bit more difficult to improve upon, but not impossible. There's no time to start like the present. There are numerous people who built their platform from the ground up.

In the first section, we introduced ourselves by sharing our bio. Bob has a strong platform from his days as a Green Beret. Jen's background is in business, so she had to build her platform a little differently. Notice her fascination with the darker side of human nature. She's building her platform based on local infamous murders that have taken place in her hometown and her study of those criminals. Platform is becoming known as something. She is becoming known as the romance author with a hint of darkness.

If your platform is weak, become known as THE writer of that type of book. That's platform. With the Internet, instead of becoming broader, things have become more niche. Being niche gives you a greater chance of finding your specific readers. With *Duty, Honor, Country*, Bob can focus on finding readers among West Point graduates and people who are interested in the Civil War.

Promotion is often hard, as one Myers-Briggs INFJ character type is labeled 'author' while the exact opposite, ESTP, is labeled 'promoter.' We HAVE to get out of our comfort zones as authors. In Write It Forward we emphasize doing the *opposite* of your Myers-Briggs personality type. It's easy to do what comes naturally. It's much harder and requires Change and Courage to do those things which make us uncomfortable.

The advent of social media is a boon to writers. We can actually do promotion from the safety of our offices. However, before you begin a major promotional campaign, it is important to figure out your platform and your product (content) first. Too many authors leap blindly into social media and we watch 95% of them wasting their time and energy flailing about inefficiently. Everything you do on social media comes back to you, the brand. Do you have your book cover as your avatar on Twitter? A picture of your cat? Fughhedaboutit. Your avatar is your head shot, because *you* are your brand, not the book.

The bottom line is, as a writer, you have to evaluate yourself on the three P variables and figure out what type you are. Then approach the business accordingly, while at the same time, working hard to improve in those areas where you are weak.

So let's take a look at this with the release *The Jefferson Allegiance*.

Platform: West Point graduate, former Infantry and Special Forces officer, bestselling author of factual fiction.

Product: A military based thriller steeped in fact from both history and present day to blend fictional elements making an exciting read.

Promotion: Newsletter, Reviews, Paid placement in print (Military Mags), discuss and work with eBookstores for placement (an exclusive release for one month with PubIt for product placement on blog).

The Result: Hit number 2 nationally on the Nook.

Bob Mayer and Jen Talty

SECTION THREE: THE DIGITAL PROCESS

A lot goes into the making of a novel. It's a long, drawn out process from idea to computer screen to marketable product. The digital book has made it easier for authors to reach their readers. The digital book can go through production quicker and the time from the actual completion of the eBook to the time it takes to become available for download is sometimes less than twenty-four hours. But that doesn't mean an author should cut corners. There is the old argument about what is more important, the beginning of a novel or the end? The beginning is important because if you don't hook the reader, they won't get to the end. However, if the ending is less than satisfying, then the reader won't be buying the next book.

The entire process is equally important and not only will an author have to put in the time to write the book, but there are expenses to being an indie author, despite what you might see people touting on the Internet. There are expenses to being a traditional author. There's no way around it. Many traditionally published authors will end up paying for promotional items, from pens to sticky notes to attending conferences to buying their own books to give to reviewers, bloggers or as a prize in a contest. All those things cost money. All of these expenses are part of the cost of doing business and every author, no matter the path, is going to have some expenses.

However, in traditional publishing your covers and editing are included in your deal. With self-publishing, the cost to edit your book and to create a cover is one the author is going to have to include in their cost of doing business.

No matter how good a writer you are, you will need, at the very least, a proofreader or a copy editor.

Your cover is your number one marketing tool. It's important that it says something about the genre and tone of your book. You'll also use your cover in promoting so it needs to be something that really pops.

Both editing and cover design are key components to being a successful indie author.

A book, no matter the format, is a book. However, a digital book is different from a print book in many ways.

FORMAT

The most obvious is format. With the printed book, you basically have Hardcover, Mass Market Paperback and Trade Paperback. The book must be formatted for the printing press, something the publisher handles. In traditional publishing, a print run is predetermined based on pre-orders and the author's sales numbers from previous sales. If it is the author's debut book, the print run is generally based on the size of the advance, which is predetermined by the publisher based on what they estimate the sales number will be.

Print on Demand technology is revolutionizing the self-publishing industry, making it easier for the author to have smaller print runs, if they have print runs at all. It costs as much to print one book with POD as five thousand. POD formats the Print-On-Demand book based on specs provided by the self-publishing company. Thus, the author can order as many or as few copies as they need.

With companies like Createspace (Amazon) and LuLu and Lightning Source, it is a very simple process to make a print book, but will anyone carry it? Bookstores will not carry most self-published or even small press books. It used to be that Borders was relatively friendly toward local authors, regardless of self-publishing, or small independent presses who used Print-On-Demand technology, but Borders has gone out of business. Even Amazon is finding it difficult to break into the "print" business since many of the independent bookstores will not carry their books.

The shift to digital has begun. Not because of technology. The technology has been there for over a decade, but because the consumer has spoken and the devices to read the books on have arrived in massive quantities. Many people who buy books are using eReaders and downloading. Yes, there are still people who buy the printed book, but from where? Online bookstores and stores like Target. You won't be seeing your POD (Print on Demand) book in your local grocery store any time soon, but your POD titles can be listed on sites like Amazon and Barnes and Noble.

We have found that 99% of our sales for fiction are in eBook format. For non-fiction our sales are roughly 50% POD and 50% eBook. For a self-publishing fiction author, your focus should be on the eBook, because that is where you will have distribution.

The digital book is different because it is a file that is downloadable onto different devices. You have two basic file types. Mobi (Kindle) and ePub (all the rest). Technology has made it relatively easy to create an eBook, upload it to Amazon through KDP (Kindle Direct Publishing) or PubIt (Barnes and Noble) and other similar sites. But here is the big problem with the "ease" of creating an eBook: Many authors believe all you have to do is use something like Calibre and convert a PDF into various formats and upload. Or simply upload a Word document to PubIt! or Kindle. Or use Smashword's "meat grinder" with a "clean" Word document and there you go--instant eBook. Except, authors are not programmers and often times the code generated from programs like Word creates enough garbage that the conversion process becomes unstable.

How often have you read an eBook on Kindle and it has many hanging indents? Or blank pages? Or hyphens everywhere? Or extra spaces where there should be only one? Or you don't have the ability to change font size? This is in part due to the author not following specific formatting guidelines, but it is also due to the HTML code that you can't see in Word which often translates into bad formatting. We've experienced it first hand.

From a technical standpoint, it's best to use programs like InDesign to create a quality eBook. However, that is not always possible and there are other options that will create just as good a product. What authors need to consider is that just because you can do this quickly, doesn't mean you should cut corners. If you do choose to create the eBooks yourself, then take the time to learn the ins and outs and avoid using Word's .HTM. We will get more specific in formatting in the next chapter.

DRM OR DIGITAL RIGHTS MANAGEMENT

DRM is a technique that restricts what the end-user can do with your eBook. It can prohibit ownership transfers, sharing or lending of the eBook and even limit how much you can print (if at all) of the eBook. The idea behind DRM is the prevention of pirating the eBook and protecting the publisher and their authors. However, DRM can cause the buyer of the book a few problems. It can restrict access to the book from other devices or limit how many devices you can read the eBook on. This can be a problem for someone who reads on their Kindle, iPad, computer and mobile phone. Also, DRM can cause the book to be lost if an end-user updates or upgrades one of their devices. We no longer use DRM on our eBooks. We participate in lending programs. We want our readers to be able to access our books, even if that means they "borrowed" it from a friend. That friend, if they love the book, will purchase other books.

Piracy is an issue many authors are up in arms about. We recommend not wasting your time trying to fight it. Those who are willing to pirate a book are going to find a way to do it. It's almost a compliment if people feel the need to pirate your book. The vast majority of your readers will buy the book.

Updating

Digital publishing also differs in that it can be easily updated. When readers said they wanted the book to end closer to 100% complete versus what some publishers are doing at 65% (filling the rest with ads and excerpts), we did a double check of our books and made some minor adjustments. We also redid some of the excerpts and as the technology has gotten better, we've made the eBook reading experience better by updating our books to meet the new standards. We are currently adding video to some of our books to enhance Bob's teaching. Updating the printed book would be costly, but with eBooks it's relatively easy.

Long tail

A key element with digital publishing is the long tail. We discussed *The Jefferson Allegiance* and its fantastic rise to #2 nationally on the Nook. Now that it has fallen off the lists, with traditional publishing, the book would be dead. In the digital world, however, the book is never dead. Print publishing pushes everything in volume sales in the first two weeks of release. If it doesn't stick, it's done. The publisher moves on and frankly, so does the author because why promote a book that the publisher isn't backing? But with digital and indie, things are different. *The Jefferson Allegiance* continues to rack up sales, and as we uploaded it to more platforms after its exclusive run on PubIt, the sales have surged back up.

Clickable links

Also, in digital, you can link things. Many eReaders have the ability to connect with the Internet, so you can easily link to something important without ruining the reading experience. For example, if you are reading this on a device such as an iPad, Kindle, Nook or Kobo eReader, here is a link to a Huffington Post article on Print Publishing versus Digital Publishing. Go ahead, click the link, take your time, read the article, we will be here waiting...

Those of you reading this in the print edition, this link (http://www.huffingtonpost.com/2011/08/10/digital-publishing-print-_n_923307.html?) will also be Appendix A.

There is a caveat to putting links, media, etc. in eBooks. For non-fiction, we believe almost anything goes as long as it enhances the subject matter. But for fiction, you need to be careful. Readers don't want to be pulled from the story. However, with proper analytics you can "see" if your readers are clicking to the link. This way you can figure out what works in your links and what doesn't.

We originally planned to make *Duty, Honor, Country* an enhanced eBook. However, after putting maps, photos and hyperlinks to additional information on historical information in the book, we found it tended to take away from the flow of the story. There will be popular enhanced novels, but we believe authors need to be very careful about distracting their readers. For fiction, we recommend any video or links to be placed as a supplement and labeled as such in the table of contents.

Marketplace

A mantra at Write It Forward is writers produce the product, readers consume the product and everything else is in between. Five years ago, this wasn't as true. When Jen first published it was with an ePublisher that was venturing into Mass Market. Unfortunately, the company went bankrupt, but the key concept was that many of these ePublishers were looking to get into the print business because that was where the majority of sales were being made...in bookstores. Even if readers weren't actually buying in the store, but online, it was the physical book they were purchasing. The eBook business was a small population of readers. We know that has changed drastically, and so has the reach each author has to their reader. You constantly see statistics thrown about defining the percentage of print vs. eBook sales. We question not only the validity of these numbers (since no one is counting our hundreds of thousands of eBook sales) but also their applicability to most authors. What skews the numbers toward print sales is the #1 retailer of print: Wal-Mart. Add in Target and Costco, and you have a considerable number of print sales. But whose books are they selling? Only the top 1% of authors. For most authors, eBook sales are outstripping print sales simply because eBooks have greater distribution.

Quantifying the digital marketplace is almost impossible right now because the data is changing too quickly to keep track. The core customer has not really been defined. The avid reader will buy a device like a Kindle. The people buying devices like the iPad and the new KindleFire or Nook tablet are not necessarily avid readers, although we could argue that Kindle and Nook are dedicated more to the reading experience than the iPad just because of who makes the product.

The eBook market is very different, but the key issue is discoverability. We're going to discuss this later on, but for now, it's important to understand how the eBook market currently works. More importantly, to accept that the eBook market is constantly evolving. Look at any product that is technology related, like computers, laptops, mini computers, car phones, cell phones, smart phones. It all evolves and the digital book is in its infancy stage. The end user is also still developing and changing what they want. Consider how Netflix went from primarily mailing DVDs to directly streaming shows and movies.

There is only one absolute right now in publishing and that is digital publishing is a game changer for authors.

Rethinking an Author's Career Path

Almost un-noticed in the 'gold rush' of self-publishing and the obstinacy of traditional publishing to cling on to the old ways has been the fact that writers really need to re-evaluate what it means to have a career as an author.

The traditional route was:

Write a book. Get an agent. Agent sells to editor. Editor promotes in-house. Sales reps place books in stores. Stores sell books to readers. Hope for an explosion out of the gate with hitting a bestseller list (only possible, though, if enough books have been placed, which rarely happens for new authors). Wait six months on numbers. Up or out. 90% out.

In essence, you had to go to bat and hit a homerun on your first swing. There was also a place for the midlist author to swing away hitting singles and doubles for years before finally getting that opportunity to hit that homerun but it was more likely that you eventually hit strike one (it didn't take three strikes) and you're out of the game.

That's all changing. First, the midlist is becoming extinct as retail outlets disappear. Second, the bestseller lists are crowded with the usual names as publishers focus on known, brand name authors, who make 90% of their money.

So now we have a rush, a gold rush as the *Washington Post* called it, or simply a pile of gold known as backlist, according to *Forbes* (http://www.forbes.com/sites/booked/2011/05/18/is-there-gold-in-your-backlist-self-publish-and-find-out/) where Bob was quoted. While the latter has some validity, the former is very misleading if you want a career as an author, which we define as making a living off of your writing.

The Amanda Hocking model is, in essence, much like the JK Rowling model. An aberration that you shouldn't spend much time studying, other than for the smart lessons she's passed on about things she did to help sell books.

What we're seeing is that 95% of those who go the indie publishing route want instant validation and gratification. That's no different than the percentages when print on demand first became available. In 2006 there were 1.2 million titles available. And 950,000 of those titles sold less than 99 copies. The percentages are little different now with eBooks. This is a harsh reality you need to be aware of.

Almost all the talk in indie publishing is about promotion and sales, when it really should be more about craft and writing. Becoming a better writer is the #1 way to improve sales.

Instead of a gold rush, consider it a marathon. Instead of rushing books out and checking your Kindle sales every day, hoping to see money pouring in, focus on the writing. The 'long tail' is the key to success as an indie author and that is why there is gold in backlist. In 2011, Bob's *Atlantis* and *Area 51* series were our bread and butter.

Bob has reached and passed the point where he can be self-sustaining financially, simply based on his backlist. Thus, writing forward, projecting out successful series, is icing on the cake. His first original book straight to eBook, *Chasing The Ghost*, remained on the top 10 Men's Adventure list for months. For a new writer, with no backlist, you have to think in terms of many books, not just one or two. Don't worry about sales now. Worry about writing better books. Building your readership, slowly but surely. Establishing a line of books that will have your readers anticipating the next one coming out. Perhaps consider writing shorter books, 50-60 thousand words, rather than the usual 80-100 thousand. Keep building community via social media.

EDITING

Let's talk about different ways to make sure your book is the best it can be.

Content editing and Beta Readers

We love beta readers and both of us are lucky that we have found good beta readers. People who will be brutally honest. We trust these people to tell us where characters and plot are falling apart. We listen to them. We don't follow them blindly, but we listen. Beta readers can point out problems, but rarely can they give you the solution to the problem. You own the book and you know its entirety.

In traditional publishing this is our main editor. The one we work with during the writing process. The one that tells us a character isn't working, or a scene is lacking, or the plot is falling apart. There is a trust that goes into working with editors and that same trust needs to apply with beta readers.

There is a tendency for writers to use other writers for beta or content editing. We don't recommend doing this unless the writer can separate themselves from the writing and simply read the story and give feedback on character and plot.

Other writers are great for brainstorming and hashing out characters and plot before the writing, or during the writing process. But authors, when reading a manuscript, tend to focus on the different aspects of the "writing" and not necessarily on the "storytelling." A writer tends to catch all the dangling modifiers and misuse of words and this takes the focus off the story. We prefer beta readers over a critique group full of writers. Often, writers will get too caught up in the minutiae of the craft and not focus on the overall objective of the book.

Never send your manuscript to people who love to stroke your ego. It doesn't help make the book the best it can be. No matter how great a writer you are, you need feedback. You need people who will tell you their emotional gut reaction to your story and your characters.

On the other hand, never send your manuscript to people who love to destroy your ego. A content or beta reader's opinion will be on the story and how it made them feel, which characters they liked, which aspects of the plot made them sit on the edge of their seat, turning the page, unable to stop, or which parts were predictable and perhaps boring. They can tell you how they felt about the beginning. When it really hooked them. And they can tell you about how they felt after they finished the book. Those who love to put us down will only focus on the negative and tell you why the book will never be good enough.

Give your book to the people that have a tendency to make you go "argh, they just don't get it," because those people are the ones who really "get it." You want more than one reader, but most likely no more than three. Ever hear the expression "too many cooks spoil the soup?" The same is true for your writing in the sense that too much feedback can overwhelm you. Blindly following any feedback can dilute your story. Your beta readers may say different things, but try to search for common threads in their comments.

One of the things Bob teaches in Write It Forward is that anything that makes you angry is the one thing you need to focus on. If, when getting feedback from your beta readers, something they say makes you unusually upset or angry, that is the thing you really need to look at closely. We have a hard time letting go of bad writing.

You've heard the phrase "kill your darlings?" There is a part of the book that you are emotionally attached to that needs to be cut. The reason you're emotionally attached to it is that exact reason: your conscious mind is defending something your subconscious knows needs to go.

The bottom line is you have a story to tell and only you can tell that story. The mature writer will know in their gut when they need to change something. It is instinctual and we have to learn to trust that instinct.

Character development and plotting are a huge part of writing a book. Often it is the most important, but that doesn't mean we are off the hook with the fine tuning of the words on the page.

Copy editing and Proofreading

Find a good copy editor. Don't use your beta readers. You want fresh eyes so they can catch all the mistakes. Your beta readers will have already read the manuscript, and even though you most likely made changes, they will have been predisposed to the words and they will miss mistakes. Also, you run the risk of them becoming upset if you didn't make the changes they suggested.

You also want to hire a copy editor who won't be focused on story, but strictly on the words on the page. You want someone who will focus on word choice, grammar and fact-checking.

You could also use a proofreader. Understand a copy editor is different from a proofreader because a copy editor will pick up sentence structure and style where a proofreader will find common grammar and spelling mistakes. You have to trust your proofreader and copy editor.

At Who Dares Wins Publishing we have contracted a former editor from New York along with two different copy editors.

There are a variety of services on the internet that list editors and copy editors. Do your homework. When hiring anyone, ask for a client list. Ask to see work they've done. Ask for references. Check out their background. Where have they worked as an editor? Have they only done freelance? Or worked for publishing houses or perhaps in technical writing?

Compare pricing with other services and with other authors who have hired different editors. The most expensive doesn't always mean the best. The cheapest, though is usually not the most qualified.

What about a book doctor?

If you don't have good beta readers, you can always hire someone. Caveat. Get to know them. Ask for credentials and a list of clients. Are any of their clients published by a New York publisher? Self-published and, if so, how successful are they? Ask them for a sample. You might have to pay a deposit, but it is important to trust the person you hire to edit content. Also, make sure the book doctor or paid editor is in your target audience. Yes, good writing is good writing, but we all have personal preferences and genre writing needs someone who understands the genre.

Another thing to consider is how much they "doctor" your book. Bob has done paid critiques before and he only does a one page cover letter (idea), one page synopsis (story) and the first ten pages (writing style). Basically, a submission critique for what you'd send to a publisher or agent. He can point out what is wrong in the writing in the first few pages because he is an expert at writing. He also asks questions in your manuscript about why you did something.

But Bob is not a book doctor. A book doctor will break apart your entire book and tell you why they think it hasn't sold to New York, or how you could improve on the entire book so it will sell.

In the past, a book doctor was considered a dirty word in the world of publishing. Today, not as much. Every author, no matter how talented, needs a content editor of some kind. In a way, good beta readers are content editors.

All too often we see writers with no real experience in any form of publishing offering their services to other writers. They toss out all these big writing terms and tell you exactly what you need and practically guarantee you a New York contract or mega-sales. When you see them, run. Fast. No one can guarantee you either of those things.

If you choose to go with any form of book doctor or paid editor, as with anything, trust your instincts as a writer. The bottom line is you had a vision when you started, and it's *your* book.

Prep for Publication

Once you have your book edited you will want to make sure the file set up looks professional. In digital publishing it is important not to load your front matter with too much information. The cover, a copyright page and a title page are all that is necessary. As with end matter, putting too much in the beginning bothers readers. Also, if you do *look inside the pages*, all the reader is getting for a preview is front matter and not the book itself.

The way we handle end matter now is to put in a few product descriptions and links to the appropriate eBookstore page. This means that we need to create files for each vendor and insert new links each time, but readers do click on those links.

We've also started inserting a short video of Bob's appearance on the Discovery Channel as a former Green Beret. We are doing this in his Green Beret Books to give readers a sense of what it is really like.

This does not take up much space and is linked in the Table of Contents.

Having a linked Table of Contents is critical, even for fiction books. Readers like them. It's the eReader way of fanning through the pages. There are various ways to generate a Table of Contents. Using Word's "insert TOC" doesn't work with eBooks, and bookmarks can create problems so it's best to use them inside an HTML editor. Programs like InDesign and Pages have a TOC generator that works really well when creating a TOC for an eBook.

Title and Cover

"A picture is worth a thousand words." A picture can tell a story just as well as descriptive text.

The best promotion is a great book, but the number one immediate marketing tools you have are your cover and title.

Title is important.

Bob looks at the titles for his six books now and he cringes. There is little in the title of any of those books to interest the reader. What does *Synbat* mean to you? You knew it stood for Synthetic Battle Form, right? And you know what a *Cut Out* is in covert operations, correct? Not only don't you know what those titles mean, you're not even sure what type of book it is, what genre it represents.

So then why should readers pick up those books or check inside the covers online to see what it's about? Do that yourself. Go to the bookstore and just scan. Or go to Amazon and look down lists of books. Besides the cover art (if the book is fortunate not to be spine out in the physical bookstore), what do you notice? The title. And which ones catch your interest? It is something very important to think about and consider.

Mary Higgins Clark says the title should invite you into the book. Many authors come up with a title that only makes sense if you read the book (i.e. the title comes out of the book). But that's backwards logic. Because no one is going to read the book unless the title draws them in. We recommend spending a considerable amount of time thinking about your title. We believe it is the #1 immediate marketing device the writer has control of.

Title should work one of two ways: It should entice the reader by giving a clear idea what the book is about (i.e. *Clear and Present Danger* signals the book is a thriller). Or be a juxtaposition of words that don't belong together and therefore intrigue the reader: *Lovely Bones.*

Cover

Cover can make or break a book, especially for online buying. In a bookstore, most books are racked spine out, so author name and title means more. Readers can pick up your book, thumb through, get a feel for story and writing and then decide. Online, readers see your cover. It has to say, "Buy me, I'm a good book!" to the reader. If it doesn't, why would they take the time to possibly download a sample, or even look at product description? It also has to indicate the book is professionally done, especially with so many people self-publishing.

If you are designing your own covers you need to consider four things: Where are you going to get your images? Do you know basic design concepts? Do you have the proper tools? *And* do you know how to use them?

Stock photo sites such as Shutterstock (http://shutterstock.com) and iStockphoto (http://istockphoto.com) are great resources for images. Most of the images are royalty free, meaning you pay a one time usage fee for the image. However, there are some images that cannot be used, so check the licensing and usage information before downloading.

We don't recommend using images you find on the Internet because the person who created the image copyrights most of them, although there are some images that are in the public domain.

One thing that drives Jen crazy is when someone says it looks "photoshopped." Photoshop is a very powerful tool and when used properly, it's difficult to tell when images have been manipulated, or blended, etc. But if someone who doesn't know how to use Photoshop or other programs like it utilizes the software, then it simply looks amateurish.

There are many programs to choose from. There are many do it yourself programs, free programs, even programs that come with your computer that can create cover design. Even Word has the capability of designing a basic cover, but will the cover be good enough to invite the reader in? It's worth your time and energy to do it right. Will it look professional? Readers might not check who the publisher is for a book, but an amateurish cover is a huge turn off.

We made the decision to invest in the proper tools to do it ourselves because we had the design background, and the technical ability. We purchased the complete InDesign package from Adobe ($1,299.00), which includes Photoshop. We also chose this program because of the ability to create full cover jackets for print books and it also has Dreamweaver, a powerful website tool. InDesign also has the ability to create ePub files that pass the quality assurance test for iBooks and Kobo.

The other thing you have to consider is your time. Being a cover artist, Jen can tell you that sometimes she hits the jackpot right away. Other times, it will take her days or weeks to get it right. As we've said before, the best promotion is a good book. Better promotion is another good book, which will need another kick-ass cover. Do you have the time and expertise to keep creating quality covers or would it be better to outsource it?

If you do choose to create the cover yourself, we recommend asking for input from impartial people. We've done this on a place called Kindleboards (more on this and Nookboards later). We've posted various cover combinations asking what people think, especially if we are on the fence about a cover. We did this for *Area 51 Nosferatu* and we've very glad we did. We found out that the image we had was used in various cartoon comics along with a few video games. Also, the reaction was overwhelmingly negative. We opted for a different image. One that gave the feel we were looking for and the reaction has been much more positive.

You do have to take things in stride when asking for opinions. We're not sure why, but often people are more apt to criticize. It is important to be able to wade through the comments and embrace what makes sense. That doesn't mean only listen to those people who like it. If a comment makes you angry, perhaps that anger is telling you something important.

There is a creative process to cover design. Jen will spend hours combing the stock photo sites for various images. She will then create four to five very different cover mock-ups, keeping in mind the over-all branding strategies, to send to Bob or any of the other authors she is working with. It is then a back and forth process where the author is giving input and Jen is doing what is possible to make the vision of the author's story make sense in the vision of the cover. It is truly a collaborative effort. We don't rely only on Jen's abilities, as good as they are, but we rely on the author's unique ability to see their book in Jen's design. Once we do that, we've hit pay dirt.

Hiring someone to do your covers can run as low as $50 and as high as $1,000. We always tell people to beware of those who charge too little and those who charge too much. Do your research. Look at the covers they've designed. Ask for references.

It's not unreasonable for a cover artist to ask for a non-refundable deposit to hire them. When Jen does contract work for cover designs she asks for a non-refundable consultation fee of $50. She does this because sometimes authors will decide they don't want her covers and this at least compensates her for the initial work up front.

Also, a cover artist's work is copyrighted. You have paid for the right to use their design for your book. In turn, you are generally required to give the artist credit for their work on the copyright page.

Whether you create the cover yourself, or you hire someone, there are some key things that go into the making of a cover for an eBook. These are not necessarily the same for a print book.

Also, remember with an eBook you don't have inside cover flap copy (hardcover) or back cover copy. That material goes into your product description.

Professional looking

If the cover looks as if you just tossed a few things together, then the reader will most likely have a negative reaction and not buy the book. One thing that stands out as amateurish is when the author uses someone they know to do "art-work" for the cover and the person isn't a professional graphic artist. Hand-drawn images that are scanned rarely work.

Pop In Thumbnail

Your cover must be readable in an image size that is 100x150. The image on the cover must be recognizable and preferably the author name and title should be legible, so the font choice is very important. There is such a thing as being overly creative. Simple is almost always better.

Go to Amazon or Barnes and Noble and look at covers. Look at books published five years ago and look at books published today by the same authors. One thing we've noticed is even New York is seeing their images have to be different to sell books online. Physical books can have raised lettering and different textures to lure the reader in. It's also larger than what is on the computer screen, so the designer can focus a lot more attention on image and not on title and name.

Another difference with the eBook and the print book are cover quotes. You can't read them on the eBook cover in thumbnail. Some authors will argue that the quote adds legitimacy to the book, especially if the quote comes from a brand name author such as James Patterson. However, we put these types of quotes in our product description and inside the book. They really are more apt to be read that way. On a thumbnail sized book, these things tend to just clutter it up.

Contrast

One of the things we learned early on was the importance of contrast in both color and image. If the cover has a dark background, you need lettering that will stand out. Many authors tend to use similar colors for background and for title. They do this because they don't want to take away from the image, but it makes the title difficult to read. Even worse, the author's name then becomes unimportant, and as we have mentioned throughout this book, the author is the brand.

If things blend too much, then your cover could easily be passed over for something more enticing. If you have a white background to your cover, it will fade into the page on which it's displayed, losing the effect of appearing to even be a cover.

Most designers will try to use a four-color scheme in the designs. This gives you more options with contrasting.

Must say something about the book

When we were first coming up with the cover for *Duty, Honor, Country: A Novel of West Point and the Civil War* some of the feedback we got was that it looked too much like non-fiction--except that was exactly the response we wanted. While the book is fiction (look at the title..."A Novel"...) it is based in fact (Bob writes Factual Fiction).

For Jen's romances, the emphasis needed to be on the suspense aspect more than the romance aspect, so we went with something that created a hint of darkness to each cover.

Consider Branding

Each book an author writes is an extension of their brand. We will cover branding in detail in **Section Four** under **The Branding Plan**, but it is important to mention it here because the cover can and will become an important aspect of your brand.

Are all your books going to be the same?

Mary Reed McCall (http://maryreedmcall.com) writes Medieval Romances. Her covers are going to change, but there are a few distinct things you can do to make all your covers connected.

One of the things we did with Mary's books was make the images singular and keep the exact font on every cover. Here is *Secret Vows*, the first book of Mary's we published.

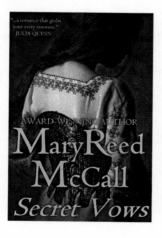

Now let's take a look at *The Crimson Lady*. Notice the background. It's similar, but a different color. Also, the lady in the image has her back facing out, just like in the first cover.

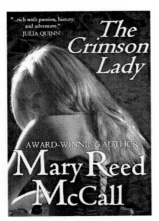

For *The Templar's Seduction* we used a male image vs. the female because the book is centered more closely on the hero. Notice that his back is also facing out, and once again we used the same font. The background is different, but they all don't have to be the same. These covers echo each other so that when a reader sees them the author's name will register.

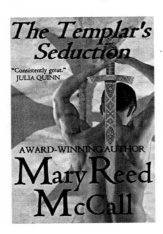

Creating Covers for Series and Multi-Published Authors

Bob Mayer is a prolific writer and not just in one genre, but many. He's had two successful series in science fiction. He's also had successful series in thrillers, military thrillers, and romantic adventure, and has written many non-fiction books for writers. It makes branding through covers very difficult. Then again, Bob Mayer is the brand, but we had to start somewhere.

Let's take a look at what we did with the *Area 51* Series.

 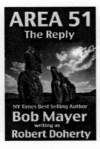 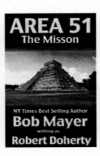 

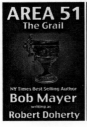    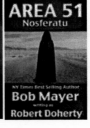

It's important that you tie the covers together with something unifying. It can be an image or simply the placement of name and title as we did above. It's clear that all these books are similar--a series.

And since we're talking about branding, one other thing we've done if you look at all the images, there is something somewhat factual about each one. *Area 51* and *Area 51 Nosferatu* have the same background image but using a different color tone and a different sky. It's the road that leads to Area 51. We have the images from Easter Island, a Pyramid, The Sphinx, The Grail, Excalibur, Stone Hedge and the Earth. All are tangible objects.

We had to be mindful of the fact that these books were originally published under the name Robert Doherty, so we put that name on the cover as well.

Cover is often the first impression the reader will get of your work. It also sends a message, not just about the book or series, but it will trigger a memory response when a reader sees something similar.

The goal with branding is to make it part of the creed that comes with being a Bob Mayer release.

When we run Facebook or Google ads, the cover will appear in the ad off to the side of the page. While you get few actual clicks on the ad, it can appear hundreds of thousands of time. It is important to realize that your cover impression weeds its way into the subconscious via peripheral vision, so something striking and simple is best.

One thing to be careful of when trying to pull everything together and being similar is that too much of a similarity could be a bad thing. It is important to break things up a bit. Let's take a look at the Green Beret Series by Bob Mayer.

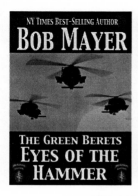

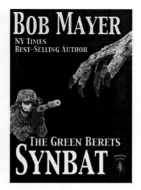

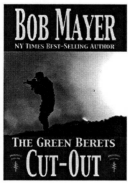

The Green Beret Series is a military thriller series, but we wanted to brand them under the Bob Mayer name, so we made them similar in style with a similar font. We also added the Special-Forces Airborne patch to each one. However, note there are some differences. Two patches on *Eyes of the Hammer* and *Cut Out*. One on the rest. The center color on *Synbat* fades into the bar colors on top and bottom. On *Z, The Green Berets* is offset on the letter because of the shortness of title.

With Victoria Martinez, the goal was to create a certain feel with her books. As you can see, Volume I and Volume II have a similar chair but the coloring is different. *The Royal W.E.* is a different book all together, but if you liked the other two, you would enjoy this unique glimpse into Royal life.

If Victoria were to write something outside Royal History, we would consider doing something very different with the covers, but if the book were related in some way, we would try to pull in key elements. For example, Victoria is teaching a workshop on how to research both fiction and non-fiction books. When that develops into a book, keeping the font the same might be a good idea, but putting her name at the top and the title at the bottom might help separate the subject matter. The image would also be a key element in making the books different, but recognizable as a Victoria Martinez brand.

All of the covers we've shown you so far have simple images. There have been some alterations to color tones. In Victoria's Volume II cover, the purple on the arms of the chair were originally pink. In *Cut Out* by Bob Mayer, we took out the soldiers that were in the original image and replaced them with the silhouette. Superimposing images can be relatively easy if you know what you are doing, but there are many other techniques you can use to get the right look and feel for your book.

The Jefferson Allegiance cover took a long time to create. It is three images blended together as one. There is the picture of Thomas Jefferson, the picture of the soldier and then the picture of the explosion in the background. The soldier and the flames in the background were images purchased from iStockphoto while the image of Jefferson is in the public domain.

This particular book took a variety of techniques to get just right. Below is an example of poor technique of the same cover.

Here is the final cover copy. Notice not only the blending of the pictures from old to new, but we reversed the images to create the time effect since people go left to right, and Jefferson predates the modern day soldier.

As you can tell, there's a lot to consider when designing a cover for your book. It must tell the story of your book in a manner that is inviting to your target audience. It takes time to get it right, just like it takes time to write and edit your book. Since the cover is the first impression your reader has, make that impression a good one.

CREATING THE DIGITAL BOOK

You've written the book. You've had it edited and you know it's the best book possible. You've got the perfect cover and are now ready to format the document so it can be read on eReaders around the globe. So, how do you format it so the reading experience is not diminished and how do you get it into eBookstores?

When we first started digital publishing at the end of 2009, the only platform you could get into as indie author was Kindle. If you wanted your eBook in other bookstores like Barnes and Noble or iBooks you had to go through a distributor like Smashwords. Now you can get on B&N through their self-publishing arm PubIt! If you own a Mac and can create an ePub file that passes the quality tests, you can get in iBooks through a program called Producer (although Apple indicates they will be launching a program that is easier to use and more accessible). And there are other distributors, like Bookbrewer, who will, for a small royalty and fee, or a larger fee with no royalty, convert your files and distribute to Kindle, B&N, Kobo and iBooks. Starting in 2012, a new company called The Vook will give authors the ability to create their own eBooks with the option of either using the file to upload themselves, or having Vook do it for them. Jen was invited to be a beta tester for the Vook. The ability to control the creation of your eBook is very exciting. It will open a lot of doors for authors, but it is also time consuming to learn all the ins and outs of the system.

There are many companies that offer services to authors in creating both Print on Demand books and eBooks such as LuLu. These companies also offer marketing packages, premier pre-publishing packages and other services, most of which, quite honestly, are not worth the money. One-stop book publishing can be dangerous for the author. While we don't recommend that any author do it alone, we also don't recommend one-stop publishing when it comes to self-publishing.

The reality is that most of these companies offer you a boilerplate service that anyone with the same amount of money can purchase. They're not worthless, but remember the key to marketing is to find your niche, and these boilerplate promotional packages don't bother to do that. There is a fine line between a company that charges a fee to help you make money and a company that makes money by providing you with services and has no stake in you making money yourself. This is why we went with the team approach at Who Dares Wins Publishing.

Let's break this down into the main vendors and their formats. We will discuss file requirements and the best way to create the eBook for each vendor. We will also look at other aspects of uploading such as categories, metadata, etc.

As with covers you need to ask yourself if creating the eBook is something you can do. Do you have the proper tools? Do you know how to use the proper tools? Either way, having a basic understanding of the technology is key to helping you make the decision on how to proceed.

In addition to file creation, there is distribution. How will your books get in these various eBookstores?

There are many online eBookstores and there are various ways of getting in them. Each store has requirements. Some can do conversions for you, others require you to supply the proper format. We're going to break this down into how we (Who Dares Wins Publishing) handle our eBooks first and then add some other sources. We will start with the vendor and the steps it takes to get your eBook available for download. With each vendor, we will let you know the file type required and tips on how to make the best file possible.

KINDLE

If you have an Amazon account, you automatically have a KDP (Kindle Direct Publishing) account. Go to https://kdp.amazon.com/self-publishing/signin and sign in using your Amazon account. From there you will need to fill out personal information, banking information, etc. Follow the instructions carefully, especially about the banking since that is how you will get paid. If you get stuck, there are community boards that you can go to and find answers. Primary among them is Kindleboards (http://kindleboards.com). Also, there is KDP support and we have found them to be very helpful and they do respond within a reasonable amount of time. Once you have all your information set up, go to your bookshelf and click "add book" to begin the publishing process.

Book Title
The first thing you do when adding a title to Kindle is enter the book name. You then have the option to check if it is part of a series, and which volume it is in the series. This will help link all the books in your series together. One thing we do with Bob's writing books is title the series 'Writing' but we didn't put in volume numbers. This will link all Bob's writing books together during searches, but it won't put them in any order.

You can opt to put in an edition number. This helps the reader know if the book was previously published or not. Usually first edition means just that. Second edition means either it has gone from hardcover to paperback or has been updated and revised from the original.

Now it is time to enter product description, which is essential.
It's your back cover copy. The product description should invite the reader in to your novel. It should give just enough information regarding what the book is about, while raising a few questions in the reader's mind. You don't want it to be too long, nor do you want it to be too short. We recommended at least two paragraphs on the actual content of the book. We also recommend having any cover quotes, blurbs, praise or contest wins or awards in the product description. You can also put information about the entire series if the book is part of one.

You don't need to put information about the author in the product description, but it is a good idea to create an author page on Amazon. You do that by going to Amazon Author Central (http://authorcentral.amazon.com). There you can add multimedia such as blog feeds, Twitter feeds and events. You can edit and list your books and add your bibliography. This is a great way for readers to find out more about you.

The next section is the contributors.

This is where you add your author name, but you can also add other contributors. If you want or need to give credit to the book's illustrator or editor, you can do it here. The only required information is the author's name.

Next you must pick the language.

We have uploaded one book in German and two books in Spanish. We sell the books world wide, but it is important to select the correct language so that you don't confuse readers. You also have the option of choosing a publication date, name of publisher and your ISBN (International Standard Book Number). Publisher is not required. However, from a business standpoint, it wouldn't hurt to either put your name down as publisher or if you have a DBA (Doing Business As) or want to create one and use a unique company name; it will give the listing a more professional feel. We also recommend that you put in an ISBN, if you have one. This helps with the tracking of the eBook. Kindle does have its own assigned numbers, but the book business still tracks via ISBN.

We purchase our ISBN through Bowker at http://myidentifiers.com. You can purchase a single ISBN for $125.00, 10 for $250.00, 100 for $575.00 or 1000 for $1000.00, depending on what your needs are. Most books require more than one ISBN, for example: one for the print book and one for the eBook.

Next on the publishing dashboard is verifying publishing rights.

Is your book public domain? Or do you hold the publishing rights? In most cases you will hold the publishing rights. If the book was previously published, Amazon may email you during the upload process asking to see a copy of the reversion of rights.

Next is targeting your book to customers.

This is very important. The first option is categories. With Amazon you only get to choose two, so choose wisely. Before choosing your categories you might want to check out BISG (Book Industry Study Group). They have a complete list of BISAC subject headings or classification schemes. This helps bookstores classify and shelve your product. On Amazon, it helps get your book on bestseller lists. Hitting the top ten on even an obscure list betters your chances of selling more eBooks.

For example, we put *102 Solutions to Common Writing Mistakes* in the main subject heading of 'Language Arts & Disciplines,' and then sub headings of 'Authorship' and 'Composition & Creative Writing.' Authorship and Creative Writing are the two categories we are allowed, but that won't be the only lists we hit. Sales, keywords and keywords inputted by customers will determine other lists.

Next up are keywords.

You get to choose seven. Keywords are the words customers might use to search for the content that your book provides. For *102 Solutions to Common Writing Mistakes* we used: *writing, how to write, author, fiction writing, non-fiction writing, novel writing*. A comma separates the seven words, so *how to write* is considered one keyword. You can look to Google for the most common key search words that people use. You can also go to books that are similar to yours and check out the tags on the product page. Keywords are very important, so make sure they make sense and are words end users will know.

Next you need to upload your image.

You will need either a JPEG or TIFF file. Amazon does compress their images, so you don't need to. Web resolution is generally set to 72 dpi (dots per inch) and the image dimensions must be at least 500 by 800 pixels. There is a maximum of 2000 pixels on the longest side of your cover. Also, cover should be in RGB (red, green, blue), which is standard for web publishing.

The next step is uploading your book file.

This is where the fun begins. It is not as simple as browsing for your book on your computer, clicking upload and then clicking publish. There are a lot of things to consider in the actual creation of the Kindle eBook and we will go through them here.

The Kindle eBook uses a form of the Mobi file and just recently they introduced KF8 (KindleFire 8 or Mobi 8).

According to Amazon, you can use a Word document to upload. We don't recommend doing so. The best way to create a good Mobi file is to have a clean HTML file (not what Word converts to .htm or save as web page) and then on a PC use Mobicreator or on a Mac use Calibre to convert. Always use a generated TOC in either of these programs. You can create a TOC with bookmarks in Word, but that often creates blank pages if you hit the return key after creating a bookmark but before closing it. It is important to check your HTML and make sure all tags are closed and it's clean code.

(Are you getting a bit confused? Maybe this is why you need a team? Or to outsource this?)

At Who Dares Wins Publishing we create an ePub file first, then convert it to Mobi using Calibre. The ePub file is created through InDesign. You can use Pages if you have a Mac, just make sure you begin with a clean copy. While cut and paste is a writer's best friend, it's not so great when dealing with documents and creating eBooks. When you cut, you're grabbing all the coding and then pasting it into another program or new document and you have no idea how that program will react to the code.

This is the problem with uploading a Word document or a Word-generated .htm file to Kindle. The code is so bad and the file conversion so unstable you often end up with a runaway bold or hanging indents where you don't want them. Here is what bad code from Word looks like in an HTML editor.

```
5288  <p class=MsoNormalCxSpMiddle align=center style='text-align:center;text-indent:
5289  .5in;line-height:200%'><b style='mso-bidi-font-weight:normal'><span
5290  style='font-size:20.0pt;line-height:200%'><o:p> </o:p></span></b></p>
5291
5292  <p class=MsoNormalCxSpMiddle align=center style='text-align:center;text-indent:
5293  .5in;line-height:200%'><b style='mso-bidi-font-weight:normal'><span
5294  style='font-size:20.0pt;line-height:200%'><o:p> </o:p></span></b></p>
5295
5296  <p class=MsoNormalCxSpMiddle align=center style='text-align:center;text-indent:
5297  .5in;line-height:200%'><b style='mso-bidi-font-weight:normal'><span
5298  style='font-size:20.0pt;line-height:200%'><o:p> </o:p></span></b></p>
5299
5300  <p class=MsoNormalCxSpMiddle align=center style='text-align:center;text-indent:
5301  .5in;line-height:200%'><b style='mso-bidi-font-weight:normal'><span
5302  style='font-size:20.0pt;line-height:200%'>How To Get The Most Out Of A Writer's
5303  Conference<o:p></o:p></span></b></p>
5304
5305  <p class=MsoNormalCxSpMiddle align=center style='text-align:center;text-indent:
5306  .5in;line-height:200%'><b style='mso-bidi-font-weight:normal'><span
5307  style='font-size:20.0pt;line-height:200%'><o:p> </o:p></span></b></p>
5308
5309  <p class=MsoNormalCxSpMiddle align=center style='text-align:center;text-indent:
5310  .5in;line-height:200%'><span style='font-size:14.0pt;line-height:200%'>The
5311  Journey From Choosing a Conference, Attending, Bringing Your New Knowledge Home
5312  And Putting What You Learn to Work<o:p></o:p></span></p>
5313
5314  <p class=MsoNormalCxSpMiddle align=center style='text-align:center;line-height:
5315  200%'>by</p>
5316
5317  <p class=MsoNormalCxSpMiddle align=center style='text-align:center;line-height:
5318  200%'>Bob Mayer</p>
5319
5320  <p class=MsoNormalCxSpMiddle align=center style='text-align:center;line-height:
5321  200%'>and</p>
5322
5323  <p class=MsoNormalCxSpMiddle align=center style='text-align:center;line-height:
5324  200%'>Jennifer Talty</p>
5325
```

Here is what good code looks like created in an HTML editor.

```
113
114      <h1><em>Write It Forward On-Line Workshops</em></h1>
115      <p>Courses are run a Yahoo Loop and are interactive. About a week before the class you will receive an invitatic
     are posted. If you have any questions please feel free to contact either <a href="mailto:bob@bobmayer.org">Bob Mayer</a> or <a h
     All lessons are uploaded as pdf's in the file section so you can download them and print them out.</p>
116
117
118      <h1><em>Current Workshops</em></h1>
119
120
121      <h2>Sept: Conflict and Idea</h2>
122      <p><strong><em><a href="https://whodareswinspublishing.com/index.php?route=product/product&amp;path=36&amp;prod
     writing a tight book and then selling it. We'll discuss ways to find and state your original idea so that you stay on course wh
     only must conflict escalate throughout the entire novel, every single scene must have conflict in it. The Conflict Box is an ef
     lock. These two key concepts can help you focus your writing and narrow your pitch. <span class="course">Course taught by Bob f
123
124      <h2>Oct: Writing Mom's: How to do it all without losing your mind</h2>
125
126      <p><strong><em><a href="https://whodareswinspublishing.com/index.php?route=product/product&amp;product_id=100">
     media sites, continued education, volunteer for local writing group, read critique partners manuscript, research agents/publishe
     But what if you had to add: Make bottles, keep up with diaper/Gerber/ formula supplies, feed baby three times a day plus bottle
     naptime (for baby, you must write,) schedule playdates, read to baby, and hope baby actually goes to bed at the designated time
127
128      <p>For many writers, this is reality. In fact, many full-time writers are made because of a child being born. Some amazing moth
     Learn easy self study tactics, time management tips and suggestions from a ten-year freelance journalist, published author and s
129
130      <h2><strong>October/November: Blogging to Build Your Brand and Your Fan Base (this class is 40$)</strong></h
131
132      <p><strong><em><a href="https://whodareswinspublishing.com/index.php?route=product/product&amp;product_id=109">
     and a household name, blogging is probably THE most powerful tool in a writer's social media arsenal. Blogging is just part of
     build a platform of future fans. Our blogs should work for us, not the other way around.</p>
133      <p>This class will help you mine your own creative strengths for a blog that will connect you to readers. Too many u
```

If you know HTML and you can create a clean file and use Mobicreator to convert it to Mobi, then you can probably do this yourself. The question is do you have the time? It goes back to our point that the best promotion is a great book; better promotion is another great book. So writing always has to be a priority.

If you used some of the new supported formatting of KF8, then you will need to use KindleGen (a command line tool) that will generate a single KF8 file and you will then use that file to upload on your KDP dashboard (see below for more details on KindleGen and the new previewer software available for KDP users).

Make sure you look at your entire book in the preview window before you hit publish. Also, if you have the ability to look at your book on a Kindle, iPad app or any other device that has a Kindle app, we recommend you do so. We use Dropbox and then move the files into various devices before publishing to see how they look.

If you have any images in your document, make sure they are in-line and not floating. Also, make sure they aren't so large that they become difficult to adjust on the eReader.

KF8 (Kindle File 8--the next generation Mobi file)

This file has about 150 new formatting capabilities. How you create the file remains the same, however, once the basic Mobi file is created you can then convert it to KF8. We recommend reading the publishing guidelines from Amazon (http://www.amazon.com/gp/feature.html?docId=1000729511).

Amazon has a detailed instruction sheet on how to convert your files to KF8, if you've used any of the new formatting capabilities. You will need to download KindleGen and the new Kindle Previewer.

The new previewer allows you look at how your file will respond on every Kindle device. This is key to making sure your book looks its best in all digital formats.

After you've uploaded your book and previewed it, you then can click the Save and Continue button and are ready to move onto the next step.

Verifying your publishing territories

There's no reason not to make your book available worldwide unless you don't have the rights to do so. Even our Spanish and German editions are in all territories. We live in a global economy and in the age of being able to download just about anything just about anywhere, there is no valid reason not to make your books available worldwide. Amazon currently has 246 territories with 6 Amazon stores. The US, UK, Germany, France, Spain and Italy. They are expanding, creating other Amazon stores as well.

Once you select territory, it's time to set your price.

We sell the majority of our books via Amazon's KDP (Kindle Direct Publishing) self-publishing platform. Any book priced between $2.99 and $9.99 will earn the author a 70% royalty rate. If your book is priced below or above that price point, your royalty is 35%. There are some exceptions to that rule, and we will talk about pricing when we get to Marketing, but the majority of our books are priced at $2.99 or $4.99.

You can then set prices in all the new stores such as Amazon DE and Amazon Spain. The nice thing about Amazon is when they add a new territory, they automatically put your book there if you clicked worldwide rights, and they adjust the price accordingly, so you don't have to go in and manually add each new store (like in iBooks, and that is a total pain).

After you set the price, you then need to decide about Kindle Book Lending.

This will allow readers to share their purchase with a friend who has a Kindle for up to 14 days. We feel this is well worth it because if someone lends Jen Talty's *Rekindled* and they absolutely love it, they will most likely go looking for everything Jen Talty has ever written and buy it. That is a win-win situation.

Finally, you click on Save and Publish.

Once your book is live, which takes about 24-72 hours, it's perfectly all right to ask everyone you know to go over and tag your book. Actually, we recommend it. Those tags will help Amazon's computer program/algorithm know where to recommend your book and to whom. It will also add in the placement of categories. You can also tag your book. You can only tag each book once, but you can always add a tag.

Try to tag it first so people can agree with the appropriate tags. Again, make sure your tags fit your book. When you input the tag, the system shows you how relevant the tag is and offers up some suggestions. If you are wondering which tags to use, go to books that are similar to yours and see what tags they have. This is not something that Amazon will do for you.

If it's a backlist book and your out of print book still shows up on Amazon, the old reviews should link, but if they don't, you can contact Amazon and they will make sure the reviews transfer over. This also helps people understand that this is not a new book.

Reviews are very powerful. There is nothing wrong with asking people to review your book on Amazon, but it should be people who have read your book. Having all five-star reviews isn't necessarily a good thing. Readers might think it's just your friends. We've given out free eBooks asking for reviews. Most don't take the time to review it, but some will. We've also used paid review sites. Most of those reviewers will state in their review they received a free copy for the review. We've found the majority of the sites to be beneficial. The reviews have ranged from 3 stars to 5 stars.

PUBIT (BARNES AND NOBLE)

The process is very similar to Kindle. You will need to go to http://pubit.barnesandnoble.com and open a new account. Fill out all the necessary banking information, etc. and you are ready to publish on The Nook.

Once again we start with Title. Then on to List Price, Publication Date and Publisher. Then on to adding Contributors. Always list yourself first as author.

Next you upload and preview your book.

PubIt! uses the ePub file and if you have a Mac and the latest version of Pages, you can create a quality ePub file. If the document was created in Word, you will need to open it in Pages and then strip the formatting. Then you will need to import certain styles. It is best to use basic Heading 1, Heading 2, etc. before exporting to ePub. Add the cover and before exporting, click the 'use first page as cover.' It is very important to get rid of Word's coding inside of Pages or you will run in to problems.

If you are using Word, it is possible to upload your Word document and have PubIt convert it to ePub. Caveat. Word still has coding. We don't recommend (as stated earlier) using the *save as web page* option in Word and then using something like Calibre to convert to ePub. You can, and if the preview looks fine, you might be able to get away with it, but we recommend going through it page by page on the preview and then also on the device and any other device you can get your hands on to make sure there are no glitches. We have found that while it looks fine on the Nook device, there have been minor glitches on the Android smart phone. Also, while you can use a Calibre created file for PubIt, you can't use it for iBooks. It won't pass their quality assurance test.

If you have InDesign, you can create an ePub file there. InDesign, so far, is the best program we have found to create quality ePub files, but it is also expensive.

Next is uploading the image.

PubIt does have specific requirements, so you will need to make a jpeg just for PubIt. The file has to be between 5KB and 2MB and the sides of the cover need to be between 750 and 2000 pixels.

If you have an ISBN, click 'yes' and enter the number. Again, we recommend using an ISBN even though it is not necessary for Barnes and Noble and Amazon. You only need one ISBN for each eBook regardless of where you load it.

PubIt also wants to know if your book is part of a series. Barnes and Noble will link all reviews of every book in your series. This is nice because when you load the latest book in the series, shortly after it publishes, those reviews will also be listed under the new book.

They also want to know if the book is available in print, also for linking purposes, and if the book is in the public domain. You are also required to select the appropriate age group and then the book's language. Barnes and Noble will be taking their eBooks into the global market in the future.

The next question is regarding rights.

Again, there is no reason not to check worldwide rights <u>unless</u> you don't have the worldwide rights.

You also have the option of adding DRM.

We don't, but early on we did and it's something that you can't change unless you unpublish and then start over from scratch. The same thing goes for Amazon.

It's now time to pick categories.

You have five options at PubIt. Only use all five if they fit nicely with your book. An inappropriately categorized book will only upset the reader.

Keywords at Pubit are not limited by words, but by characters.

You get 100 characters, so when you use 'how to write' that uses up 12 characters.

Product Description.

You need to be a bit more careful with your description since it is also done by characters. We have run in to situations where we've had to change the product description because we didn't have enough room, so keep that in mind before publishing. You have between 200 and 4000 characters.

Author Information.

Pubit gives you a spot for information about the author. You have between 200 and 4000 characters to put in your bio and any other relevant information.

Editorial Reviews.

One thing to consider with Pubit is that they give you spots to put up Editorial Reviews. You have up to five spots, so those cover quotes and blurbs you might have in your description might be better served in these spots just for Pubit.

Finally, click 'confirm' and either 'save and keep off sale' or 'save and put on sale.' Again, it will take a couple of days for the book to show up.

PubIt pays 65%, so it's a little less than Amazon.

There is no tagging at PubIt! At least not yet. We have not seen review sites that send eBooks to reviewers like at Amazon. However, it doesn't hurt to let people know your book is available for download and that reviews are welcome.

IBOOKSTORE

The only way to get into iBooks without using an aggregator is if you have a Mac. Even with the announcement of iBooks Author (a free Mac App) you still need a Mac computer and you use something called Producer to upload your files.

The very first thing you need to do if you are going to upload directly to iBooks is download iTunes Producer and then upload eBook, cover and metadata through that. Producer gives you two choices for upload: Through the system, or bh uploading metadata using a tab-delimited file or spreadsheet. We create new packages for iBooks via the new book option.

Before you can deliver content, you must have an iTunes Connect account. You do this by going to http://itunesconnect.apple.com. This account is connected to your iTunes account.

Once you have filled out all the proper documentation, you are ready to create your first book package.

iTunes Producer

Open iTunes Producer and click on 'create new package' and then 'new book' and click 'next.' Fill in the proper information starting with ISBN. You can't load an eBook to the iBookstore without one. If you've used other sources and have gotten use of their free ISBN for your book, you cannot use it here. You must have purchased your own ISBN.

Select the language of your book and then add in the title, subtitle (if there is one), publisher, imprint, publication date, series name, number within the series, print length (if not available in print you will need to 'guess'), the BISAC Main Subject and book description. With iBooks you get to choose three categories. We use the same product description that we use at Amazon.

Once that is completed, you click on 'contributors.' Add author and any other contributors, and then click on 'related products.' If your book is available in print or audio, this would be the place to enter the relation and the ISBN numbers.

Next up...territory rights.
This is where iBooks gets a little frustrating. There are currently 32 territories. When we first loaded our books, there were six. You can use a 'default' setting, but if anything is added or you need to change, you will need to go in and change each one individually. You can do this either in Producer or through iTunes Connect under 'manage your books.'
Every territory you choose, you need to pick the publication type (we usually use digital only). You can set it up for pre-orders, but we do not use that function. You can set a physical list price but then you need to set the Tier price, which is the actual eBook list price.
Then you need to click 'cleared for sale' and check 'DRM free' if you want your books free of DRM, or don't click it if you want to activate DRM.

Then click on the next button to upload.
You upload an ePub file and, if you created it through InDesign, Pages or iBooks Author, it will meet the standards. If you created it through something like Calibre, it won't, and Producer will tell you that it wasn't loaded.
If your only desire is to publish in iBooks, then using the iBook Author App might be for you. We suggest reading the licensing agreement as it is very limiting. However, this app will allow you to

create an eBook that has multi-touch widgets, complex charts, tables and other fun things. These features are great for interactive eBooks, textbooks and other types of enhanced books, but the output created can ONLY be loaded to iBooks.

You can find out more information on the iBooks Author here: http://www.apple.com/ibooks-author.

Here is a fun YouTube video that gives a great overview of the iBooks Author (http://youtu.be/pr076C_ty_M)

You also have the option to load a preview. This is also an ePub file. This is generally a chapter or two to entice the reader. Finally, this section asks for the cover. You can use the same cover you used for Amazon. Once you've chosen the files, click 'next.'

If there is any information missing you will be told there are errors and what the errors are. You won't be able click on the deliver button until you correct these errors.

If all is good, click 'deliver' and wait. It will take a minute or two. If the book is delivered successfully, you will get a big green check. If there is a problem you will be notified. If you've hired someone to create the file, make sure you get the error information so the technical person can go back into the file and correct the mistake.

It takes about ten days for your book to start showing up. When you go into iTunes Connect and go to 'manage your books,' if there is a yellow light, it means something is missing. If that is the case, you will usually get an email from iBooks. If there is a red light, the book has not made its way to the store. If you have a green light, you are good to go.

iBooks pays 70%.

KOBO

Kobo is working on their system, and toward giving self-publishers the ability to upload directly; until that happens you will need a publisher's account in order to upload directly to their eBookstore.

The way to get your publisher's account is to go to their site (http://kobo.com) and click on 'information for authors and publisher' and they provide an email address. You will be contacted by a representative, who will help you decide which type of publishing packaging is best for you and help you set up your FTP (File Transfer Protocol) account and walk you through the steps of their metadata spreadsheet.

Right now you use something called Onix (ONline Information eXchange), which is XML metadata formats. Or you use a tab-delimiter spreadsheet to provide your metadata (WDWPUB uses the tab-delimiter spreadsheet). This spreadsheet has all the information that is required for you book such as description, pricing, territories and categories.

Then you load the spreadsheet and all your eBooks and covers through your FTP (we recommend FileZila). You will need to use BISAC codes (up to three) that will categorize your books.

Each file will need to be saved by its associated ISBN. Same with the cover, which will need to be in jpeg format with dimensions of 475 by 680.

OTHER OPTIONS

If you don't want to go through uploading your eBook on various sites you have other options.

Smashwords

Smashwords (http://smashwords.com) is a great alternative. You load it once and then you can distribute to the above listed stores along with some others. They take a small cut, but you still get a larger chunk of the proceeds.

Smashwords uses a Word doc as a source file. The key to using Smashwords effectively is to follow the *Style Guide*. Any short cuts in formatting will cause either the file format to fail when it tries to convert, or the file will not pass inspection for the Premium Catalog. This is important for two reasons. First, simple things like proper indentation for a paragraph are important to the reading experience. (Try reading a document that doesn't follow standard practice. It's annoying.) Or you may have a diagram that doesn't convert during the process because you used Word's Table function. Second, if there are any glitches in formatting, you won't make it into the Premium

Catalog and depending on where you want your eBook distributed, you won't be accepted into those stores. So, follow the Style Guide.

Bookbowker

Another distributor that we've heard good things about. They will create your files and upload. There is a fee though, where Smashwords only takes a cut of your sales. Bookbowker then takes 5% of each sale. But they also do apps and provide other services.

Vook

Jen was one of the first people to beta test Vook. The basics are you make a few minor adjustments to your Word document and then upload it to Vook. Inside Vook you add all your metadata, cover, images, tables, video and anything else you might be using inside your book.

The great thing about Vook is that it strips all but italics and bold formatting, making a clean file. You can then change paragraph styles, headings, etc. inside the system. When it comes to images or videos, you grab, drag and drop the images and video where you want them.

Once everything is created you have two options. You can have Vook distribute your eBook to Amazon, Barnes and Noble and iBooks, or you can email them to yourself and then upload to the vendors you want.

Vook is a paid service. When Jen beta tested the system, they were unsure of what the fee structure would be, but they did not plan on taking a percentage of sales, but being more of a flat-rate service.

POD services

If you want to make your book a POD, there are many services you can use. Createspace, LULU, and if you have a large number of books, Lightning Source, which is what we use. Lightning Source also distributes eBooks for us to Books on Board, AllRomance and Diesel. They also are linked with Ingram which means your book is available through that system on a pull rather than push system. What that means is that if someone wants to order a print copy, the store, whether it be on-line or a brick and mortar, can order it and sell it.

We don't recommend presses such as Author Solutions and Publish America.

Always read the fine print. Always ask other authors who they use and what their experiences have been.

SECTION FOUR: POST PUBLICATION STRATEGIES

You've written the book. Edited the book. Created a kick-ass cover for the book. Created the necessary eBook files and perhaps a print on demand book. What next?

There are a lot of things to consider. It's more than promoting a single book at a time. It's promoting a brand, and *you* are the brand. In between releases you need to be consistent in your efforts to keep yourself in front of your readers.

Even before you get your first contract or self-publish your first book there are things you can do to create community.

We've titled this section Post Publication, but these are things you need to develop and work on before publishing, during and after. Remember Bob's circle of success?

With every book you write and release, you will need to dig deep into the three Areas of Who, Dares and Wins and determine what needs adjusting, what needs to be completely revamped and then put it all together again and again, improving each time. It will be important to pull out your goals and see what you have achieved and evaluate how you will achieve the next goal. Look closely at what is working and expand on those areas. Have you developed the skills you were lacking? If not, how can you improve on your weaknesses for the next release?

The entire process is circular, not linear. Successful people continue to move forward via a circle of success because they constantly learn from the past and evaluate and plan for the future.

THE BRANDING PLAN

Every author wants to be a household name. The only way to get there is to become the author KNOWN for writing THAT kind of book. James Patterson is a brand. Nora Roberts...a brand. Remember the hit TV show "Cheers?" The bar where everyone knows your name? That is what we are trying to achieve with branding.

There is only so much room at the top. But which top are we talking about? The general top? Or a more specific top? Given the Internet supports niche, if you can hit the top of your specific niche, and have just 10,000 dedicated readers, you can have a career as a writer.

Branding is a process and it's part of your overall business plan. We go back to the beginning of this book where we mentioned if you don't know where you are going, you are likely to get lost. We see a lot of authors spinning their wheels. They're all over the place with their image. Everything you do regarding marketing and promotion is part of your overall brand. It's better to do a little well, than a lot in a scattered fashion.

We recommend reading *Primalbranding* by Patrick Hanlon. Patrick is also the founder of and CEO of Thinktopia, Inc.

The basic premise of *Primalbranding* is the "Primal Code." This code consists of The Creation Story, The Creed, The Icons, The Rituals, The Pagans or Nonbelievers, The Sacred Words and The Leader. These seven elements create your brand.

Before trying to develop the seven elements, take the time to write down your responses to the following:

Describe what you write.
Describe why you are compelled to write those kinds of stories.
Describe who would like to read those kinds of stories and why.
Describe who you think you are.
From your self-description, describe what types of people would be drawn to you and why.

Write as much or as little as you want, but when you are done, go back and look for key descriptive words. This is the foundation of building your key elements to your brand.

Let's take a look at **The Creation Story** for Crusie-Mayer. This is taken directly from the Crusie-Mayer web site http://crusiemayer.com/story.htm

One evening in Maui, Jenny Crusie was watching the sun set over the Pacific when Bob Mayer sat down beside her and said, "What do you write?" Jenny said, "Well, basically, in my books, people have sex and get married." Bob said, "In my books, people have sex and die."

Naturally they decided to collaborate. Nine months later, Don't Look Down was done.

We all have a creation story. It's part of what makes us individuals. We have one for writing too, and often it becomes a huge part of our bio. For the last year, Jen has been steadily working on the Primalbranding process for Bob Mayer, the brand.

Let's take a look at how she built his **Creation Story**.

Branding Bob Mayer. Who is he? What emotions, ideas, thoughts do we want our target readership (in fiction and non-fiction) to have?

*NY Times bestselling author **Bob Mayer** has over 50 books published. He has sold over four million books and is in demand as a team-building, life-change, and leadership speaker and consultant for his Who Dares Wins: The Green Beret Way concept which he translates into Write It*

Forward: a holistic program teaching writers how to be authors. He is also the Co-Creator of *Who Dares Wins Publishing*, which does both eBooks and Print On Demand, so he has experience in both traditional and non-traditional publishing.

His books have hit the NY Times, Publishers Weekly, Wall Street Journal and numerous other bestseller lists. *The Jefferson Allegiance*, was released independently and reached #2 overall in sales on Nook.

Bob Mayer grew up in the Bronx. After high school, he was selected to attend West Point, where he learned about the history of our military and our country. During his four years at the Academy and in the Infantry, Mayer questioned the idea of "mission over men." When he joined the special forces as a Green Beret, he felt more at ease where the men were more important that the mission.

Mayer's obsession with mythology and his vast knowledge of the military and special-forces, mixed with his strong desire to learn from history is the foundation for his science fiction series Atlantis, Area 51 and Psychic Warrior. Mayer is a master at blending elements of truth into all of his thrillers leaving the reader to question what is real and what isn't.

He took this same passion and has created thrillers based in fact and riddled with possibilities. His unique background in the Special Forces gives the reader a sense of authenticity and creates a reality that makes the reader wonder where fact ends and fiction begins.

In his historical fiction novels, Mayer blends actual events with fictional characters. He doesn't change history, but instead changes how history came into being.

Mayer's military background, coupled with his deep desire to understand the past and how it affects our future, gives his writing a rich flavor not to be missed.

Bob has presented for over 1,000 organizations both in the United States and internationally, including keynote presentations, all day workshops, and multi-day seminars. He has taught organizations ranging from Maui, to Whidbey Island, to San Diego State University, to the University of Georgia, to the Romance Writers of America National Convention, to Boston SWAT, the CIA, Fortune-500, Microsoft, the Royal Danish Navy Frogman Corps, Microsoft, Rotary, IT Teams in Silicon Valley and many others. He has also served as a Visiting Writer for NILA MFA program in Creative Writing. He has done interviews for the Wall Street Journal, Forbes, Sports Illustrated, PBS, NPR, the Discovery Channel, the SyFy channel and local cable shows. For more information see www.bobmayer.org.

When looking to build a creation story you need to ask yourself *why you exist in the eyes of your target audience. Why should people trust you?*

Bob Mayer attended West Point and was in the Infantry. While there, he took orders. He was taught mission before men. He questioned these orders and placed his men first when he became a Team Leader.

As a military man, Bob respected the men on his team, believing he did not "deserve" their respect until he earned it. He takes this same philosophy to his non-fiction and fiction work, placing the reader first.

As a Green Beret he learned to think and act in situations that were considered "lose-lose." This training has helped him survive in the world of publishing by his ability to adapt to changes. As traditional publishing began to falter, Bob stepped in to the digital and self-publishing arena. He took his skills as an A-Team leader, his ability to plan missions and his unique ingenuity to think outside the box and made the transition successfully. Bob has been successful because he looks to the past (traditional publishing) and learns from experiences so he can adapt to the future (the digital author) as it happens, instead of after it has happened.

Above all, Bob is an advocate. He is an advocate for his team members, other writers and ultimately, his readers.

Bob's fiction comes from factual aspects of his experiences with the military. In his science fiction novels, he mixes these facts with commonly known mythology (Atlantis) or well documented "rumors" (Area 51) to create a world that could exist. His military thrillers are gripping, and one has to wonder where fact ends and fiction begins. His latest endeavor, a historical fiction, blends fictional characters amongst real people such as Ulysses S. Grant and deals with such questions of loyalty and honor during the Civil War where 55 of the 60 battles were commanded by West Point Graduates on both sides.

Now, let's take a look at the second element in branding: ***The Creed.*** What is Bob Mayer's Creed?

Creed is basically a singular notion people believe. It's a log line. And it can change over time, especially as we go from one book to the next, one marketing campaign to the next. Just Do It, is a Nike creed.

Who Dares Wins: The Bob Mayer Creed.

Next up is the **Icon**. The Icon is your logo, or combination of logos. For Nike, it's the swish. For Bob we have the Who Dares Wins special-forces patch, but we also have the blue keyboard that is used on both Write It Forward and Who Dares Wins Publishing. We are currently reconsidering and re-designing our Icon to make it more unified. You have to be careful when changing an Icon if your brand is well-established. People don't adjust to change well, even when it's needed. Imagine if McDonald's changed the Golden Arches.

The key is to make the Icon fit your overall plan for branding yourself as an author. One thing we are considering is making Who Dares Wins, the Icon. Yes, you can have both the Creed and the Icon be the same. The key is to make it mean something to the reader.

Every brand has a set of *rituals* that come with it. Stephen King's ritual is fear. A ritual is a repeated interaction people have with you and your brand. In the traditional publishing model, book tours were a ritual. Now Blog Tours are a ritual. A newsletter is a ritual. A blog post is a ritual. Tweeting is a ritual. What makes it a ritual is that your readers expect it from you. This is why consistency is so important. If you had been doing newsletters six times a year and then all of a sudden just stopped, your readers would be upset, but eventually, if you didn't bring the newsletter back, you run the risk of your readers forgetting about you and then you dilute the brand.

The same goes with blogging (which we will discuss in the next chapter). If you blog and blog and blog, your readers get used to that and they come to expect it. When you stop, eventually your readers will stop coming to your blog, diluting the brand quickly and it takes a lot more to build brand than it does to destroy it.

Bob Mayer's blog readers have come to expect cutting edge information on the business of writing and Bob's unique blend of wit and humor laced in.

The Pagans or Non-Believers are ones we either like to ignore or hope we never have to deal with, but they are important parts of our brand. The old saying *bad publicity is better than no publicity*, rings true here. Think about how emotional people are when they are 'against' something. They shout it from the rooftops, creating a certain kind of buzz and people then become interested in the subject matter. What in that book is so controversial that so and so must tell us NOT to read it? Some are going to read because they have to know. Some will like it, and some will make it their sole goal to make sure no one reads your book, except that can cause the opposite effect.

We have Pagans, especially in the non-fiction aspect of Who Dares Wins Publishing. Bob has gotten attacked several times on various social media sites and writing boards for his opinions on self-publishing and traditional publishing and what the future holds. It does bother us, but on the other hand, creating that kind of stir does help us, as long as we are genuine in our belief systems. The moment you do something just for the sake of creating Pagans or for shock value, you dilute your brand and you will lose some of your believers.

Everyone wants to feel like they belong to something, especially our fans so we develop **Sacred Words**. These are specialized words that make people feel closer to you and your brand. If they know the words, they are part of the super-secret fan club. When Bob was writing with Jenny Crusie, some of their sacred words were *nothing but good times ahead; we're doomed; and living the dream*. The Bob Mayer brand consists of *Who Dares Wins, Adapt or Die, Honor VS Loyalty, Lead, Follow or Get The Hell Out of The Way*.

The final element in Primalbranding is **The Leader**. You are the leader. You are the visionary. The risk-taker. Even if you have built a team around you (like Bob), you are still the Leader and you must put yourself in that role.

Leadership is not something that everyone possesses. In Special Forces everyone had to be a leader. They had to have the ability to lead themselves. You have to help your readers follow you and join in the fun. You have to find ways to invite them into your world and to bring their friends along with them. Word-of-mouth is still the best way to sell books and it's also the best way to build brand.

Not all of these elements will be in place when you start. Also, these elements will change over time as you change and develop as an author. It's important to work on these elements constantly. We recommend writing out what you know, and keep reworking that list every couple of months. Being a successful author isn't just about writing the best book, it's also about reaching YOUR audience.

If I Build It, They Will Come; If I Write It, They Will Read It

Recently Australia's Minister for Small Business said that he believed that online sales would wipe out bookstores in five years, except for a few specialty stores.

He was greeted with outrage. From bookstore owners. "I'm gob smacked," one owner said.

Here and there, a few people are realistically saying that 99% of self-published books are going to die slow, un-noticed, deaths.

These announcements are greeted with outrage. From self-published authors.

There is a thing that supersedes these proclamations and resulting outrage. It's called *reality*.

The Australian minister made this announcement after Australia's largest book chain collapsed due to online competition. Why would someone then be gob smacked? The largest surviving chain left in the US announced it's making more off Nook sales than in-store print sales. That they were seeking shorter leases to 100 stores, to give them the "option" to close stores efficiently.

The people arguing the loudest against the rise of the eBook are independent bookstores. They claim their uniqueness and their atmosphere will keep them alive. Perhaps. But only if they adapt and provide customers with a truly unique experience. Frankly, and we know this will cause outrage, too often our experience has been in such stores of finding an attitude of "I built it, now you come in and buy some books." That attitude is reaching new heights as some indie bookstores are now going to charge customers to come in for author events. We might be wrong, but that just seems backwards. One store said that 10% of their revenue comes from this. We wonder how much of that they share with the author. In Seattle, an indie bookstore posted emails on why they declined to have an author published by Amazon do a book signing, going so far as to say Amazon was evil, and that Amazon censors books, while they proceeded to do exactly the same thing.

Many bookstores have treated genre authors as some sort of subspecies not worthy of their literary consideration. Bob literally (pun intended) has been told several times that "We don't really do your type of book" by these stores. When you don't "do" the types of books that sell the highest percentage of fiction, how do you expect to stay in business? Not only do you need readers to come to your stores, you need writers, particularly local writers and genre writers with a fan base.

What's amazing in the Seattle situation is that the bookstore was a mystery store and the author was published by Thomas and Mercer, Amazon's mystery and thriller imprint. That imprint will only grow larger over time, yet the store is saying they won't rack books by it. That is a glaring example of not facing reality. We can wish things to be different, but when we ignore the iceberg looming, it's akin to switching deckchairs on the Titanic.

Books are being loaded onto Amazon Kindle and PubIt at record numbers. The reality is, 99% will die quiet, but agonizing deaths (agonizing to the writer). At the height of the POD rush, there were 1.2 million titles in 2006. 950,000 sold less than 99 copies. At 99 cents, more writers may be selling more than 100 copies, but the income is poor and this can only last for so long. But, let's face the reality of traditional publishing: 99% of the authors who were published the same year Bob's first book came out (1991) are no longer writing for a living. It's actually probably higher than that since most weren't even writing for a living even then.

Adding to the problem, thieves are reformatting other people's books and loading them, hoping to quickly make some bucks and clogging the system. Bob's *Area 51* book was pirated and republished on Amazon Kindle like this. The fact that the thief used a character's name as the author was a red flag. We do have to give Amazon credit in that they contacted whoever uploaded the book and had it removed.

Bob did a blog post suggesting an unpublished writer should have at least three manuscripts complete before uploading, which had two reactions: On our blog, the response was overwhelmingly positive; on Kindleboards, the results were mixed, 50-50. Someone even accused Bob of trying to keep a foot in traditional publishing by suggesting writers submit to agents. As if that were some crime! We have encountered a rather negative attitude sometimes toward traditional publishing among indies, just as many traditionally published authors sneer at indies as producing drek. There's enough drek to go around in both camps. Bob has since amended that idea, and said it's okay to upload your first book on your own, but don't spend a lot of time on promotion until you have several titles to promote, otherwise you're taking the time you should be spending writing, and spending it promoting and your writing won't get any better. We will say it again: The best promotion is a good book. Better promotion is more good books.

The bottom line is just because you write it and upload it, doesn't mean many people are going to want to read it. Bob works full-time (which is week days a week, around fourteen hours a day) at being an author. Which means 50% of his time is spent running a business, and a large chunk of that is promotion. That doesn't mean running around trumpeting his books (although, let's be honest, some of it is), but rather building community and a reputation.

What is key now is that the reader-author relationship is finally the cornerstone of publishing. Authors can talk directly to their readers on social media. Bookstores had the lock on distribution for decades. They no longer do. That's a reality. To survive requires accepting that reality. Writers can now publish immediately. That's a reality. But that doesn't mean it's a good option for everyone. The successful writers are the one who realize quality content is what will draw readers, not smoke and mirrors. The best promotion is great content, and multiple titles. Success requires a long-term plan and perseverance.

Bob loves this quote from Terry Gilliam (can't beat a Python for a great line):

"Talent is less important in film-making than patience. If you really want your films to say something that you hope is unique, then patience and stamina, thick skin and a kind of stupidity, a mule-like stupidity, is what you really need."

Yee-haw.

We don't expect readers to come to our books. We have to go to the readers, with quality writing, community, blog posts, social media, conferences, unique topics, YouTube clips, answering every email, and just plain hard work.

So just because we built it or we wrote it, does not guarantee us success. Success will go to those who learn, adapt, change and work very, very hard. What we all must do is go to the READER.

SOCIAL MEDIA AND THE WRITER

The Internet has opened a world of opportunity for the writer. It has given us the ability to connect with the most important group in our community: the reader. Readers can come to our blog and leave comments and we can respond. We can visit their blogs (readers love it when their favorite authors leave a comment). We can start Twitter chats. Converse on Facebook. Post on Goodreads. Join Google+. We can DiggIt. We can Press This. Or we could StumbleUpon and if we speak Russian we can Vkontakte. At the time this book was written, Wikipedia's listing of social media sites was over a couple hundred (excluding dating sites). According to Wikipedia, this list is only of the well-known sites. They also have a list of defunct social networking websites.

Looking at the list, there are some sites that are targeted to specific types of individuals. There is a blogging community called Blogster. CafeMom, which is intended for mothers, and there is even one for baby boomers: Eons.com.

Just because there is a social media site for just about everything doesn't mean you should join it. We spend a lot of time discussing the value of our marketing efforts on our Write It Forward Blog and in workshops we teach. The Internet has given the author a wealth of ways to communicate and promote via their blog, website, Twitter (http://twitter.com), Facebook (http://facebook.com), Goodreads (http://goodreads.com), Google+ and various boards like Kindleboards (http://kindleboards.com). There are a ton of review sites, media services, best-seller campaigns and even media coaches out there with words of wisdom about how to use these sites effectively to sell books.

We all know the role of the author isn't all about just writing a better book. Every author, editor, agent and other publishing experts will tell you that you have to write a good book in order to succeed. However, that is only partially true. The good book might get you in the door and noticed by someone in publishing, or even one reader, but that is just the beginning.

Just because you wrote it, doesn't mean they will read it...

We're preaching to the choir when we tell writers they have to promote and build an internet presence, blog, tweet, Facebook, and promote their book. We're also preaching to the choir when we say sometimes we feel like all we ever do is talk with other writers. Where are the readers? We want to connect with readers.

Those who buy our fiction titles are readers. Thank you readers, now can you kindly tell me where you hang out?

Yes, we know, readers are on Facebook, Twitter and every other social media outlet known to man. We have been at this non-traditional publishing thing for two years, and while we think all the social media outlets have purpose and can be effective tools, they are just that, tools in your marketing tool-belt. The key here is to be effective.

At Romance Writers Nationals we heard a group of savvy romance writers who have hit many of the best seller lists do a workshop on social media and promotion for the author. It was an eye-opening workshop. One of the authors said that Twitter doesn't sell books, Facebook does. This was two years ago, and at the time, it was probably true. However, as with all social media sites, Facebook is undergoing some changes, and the rants Jen is hearing from her teenage and young adult children is that Facebook "sucks" and Google+ "rules." Of course, not everyone is on Google+ and Twitter still rules the universe according to many.

This brings up the key point: you can't do it all. It's better to do a few things well, than to do many things poorly, because the key is to build a brand and a community.

While we don't believe these tools have anything to do with "direct sales" we know they help create community, which over the course of time leads to sales. People who were already fans of an author will automatically follow, or join a fan page. The more you connect with them, the more they will give you the ever-elusive "word of mouth." We know people come to Write It Forward to pick Bob's brain about the craft of writing, his more than twenty years of experience in traditional publishing, and we what we're doing at **Who**

Dares Wins Publishing as we face these often scary, yet exciting changes in publishing.

If I build it, they will come....
But how do we get people to *join* us on these tools?

We're going to talk about the tools we use and have found effective. Understand that what works for one author might not work for another. There are many roads to Oz. You have to find the tools that work for you.

Blogging

Blogs are nothing new. However, more and more people are blogging. There is no shortage of experts on any given subject, and everyone is blogging about it. The key to blogging, besides being an expert, is to have purpose. Remember, purpose isn't always a specific topic.

When Bob was writing with Jennifer Crusie, their first blog was He Wrote/She Wrote which began January 1, 2006. The blog was about their Year From Hell, promoting their first collaborative book, *Don't Look Down* and discussions of their next book, *Agnes and the Hitman*. The basic concept of the blog was really a day in the life of two writers who decided to write together. That was the theme. The purpose.

The other key element to this blog was that it would end in a year. And it really did. The last post went up on December 31, 2006, and was titled: This is The End.

The blog was insanely successful in part because of their unique collaboration. Grim Former Green Beret meets the Happily-Ever-After Romance writer and together they write something...different. The Crusie-Mayer brand took off pretty quickly. Jenny brought with her "the cherries" and Bob brought his own fans.

And then came the CherryBombs...the community. The community is in part what kept this blog working. It wasn't necessarily a large community, but they took over the comment section on the blog and kept Bob and Jenny on their toes.

When the year was over, the blog ended and the CherryBombs were distraught. But Jenny and Bob created a new blog titled He Wrote/She Wrote...How To Write. The blog was also scheduled for one year. The purpose was 'how to write.' They set up a syllabus and they kept to it, and requested that the commenters to stick to the topics. At the end of the year, the blog was over and Bob and Jenny went back to their own personal blogs.

You can still find Jenny ranting over at Arghink.com and Bob now has his highly successful blog at Write It Forward (http://writeitforward.wordpress.com) dedicated to helping authors navigate all aspects of publishing.

The second HW/SW blog was very successful, but was dedicated to writing topics only. There is only so much you can blog about when it comes to writing. There is only so much you can blog about when it comes to any topic. This is in part why many authors choose to blog collectively. This can be an excellent way to expand readership and also decrease the workload on writing blogs, but it doesn't allow for the personal touch as much.

However, ask yourself how many collective blogs you go to and read?

Another thing to consider is doing what Bob & Jenny did with He Wrote/She Wrote. Since a blog is a large investment in time and writing, if you have a nonfiction area of expertise, consider making your blog a book under construction. Set out a table of contents (for HW/SW it was broken into 52 subjects, with either Bob or Jenny posting on Sunday, and the other replying on Thursday after reading all the comments in between). You could end up writing a nonfiction book via your blog, accomplishing two things at the same time, while also building your brand and your audience.

No matter how much solid content you put in your blog, you still have to make it personal to an extent, and emotional. Even at Write It Forward, Bob tries to connect with his readers on a more personal level. One of the highest commented blogs and one that got the most hits in all his personal blogs was the one where Bob decided to take Cool Gus for a ride in Puget Sound in his Kayak.

A few moments after this picture was taken, Gus jumped from the kayak to chase a whale. Lesson: don't put a six-month-old lab in a kayak.

When creating your blog, remember you can change it up. You don't have to be 'on' all the time. Some bloggers have a theme day. Others have topics and blog on those topics when appropriate.

The most important thing to ask yourself when blogging is: who is your target audience? When you can answer that question, you can then form your topics.

This brings us to the question: how do we get people to our blogs? One way is to comment on other people's blogs. Don't promote yourself or your book. Comment on their content. Be professional and polite, even if you disagree. Don't leave a link in your comment to your blog, but sign in using your WordPress or Blogger account and your name will automatically be linked back to your blog. If that won't work, most comments allow you to link your name to your website or blog.

Blogs are also great landing pages because the information on them is constantly changing. We use Write It Forward as our 'hub' of operations. We post about workshops, upcoming releases, the latest information in digital technology, and, of course, the occasional Cool Gus and Sassy Becca saga. However, we have links on the sidebar of our blog taking you to other industry professionals and our personal and professional websites.

Blogs themselves can be websites. Both Blogger and WordPress now have pages and you can use it as an inexpensive website.

Be consistent in posting. We have found that when we blog at least twice a week our blog hits and comments go up. We have also found that focusing on our readership (mostly writers) creates a community where people feel comfortable to talk amongst themselves.

Consider your voice when blogging and always be professional. Everyone is on the Internet and what you say there can and will be used against you.

Twitter

Twitter is a great social media tool and operates in "real" time. Every writer should be using some form of social media, and Twitter is one of our personal favorites, but we shouldn't be wandering around aimlessly. The goal on these sites should be to communicate thoughts and ideas to like-minded people. There is a reason hashtags on Twitter evolved — people want to talk to people who share common interests, goals, and ideals.

Twitter is great for the exchange of information. A day doesn't go by when we don't find a good link or two, or three, or five. Hashtags are great to follow streams of thought from conferences by following the conference hashtag as people tweet right from workshops and link to recaps.

We did a recap on Digital Book World based on the conversations from the hashtag (#DBW11) and links people were sharing. There are hashtags that host things like marketing chats, goal setting for writers and just about anything you can think of. While Twitter is an open forum, it's important to be respectful, and if a hashtag is used for non-promotional reasons, you should respect that. But, if you put the right information in your bio, and you communicate regularly, people will check you out.

Heidi Cohen has a great post titled *Twitter Manners Checklist,* which can be found at http://heidicohen.com/twitter-etiquette. It's worth checking out.

Here is another article from *The Guardian* in the UK that is very informative about Tweeting: http://www.guardian.co.uk/culture-professionals-network/culture-professionals-blog/2011/dec/15/twitter-rules-etiquette.

As with most things in a writer's life, balance is the key. No one really cares what you eat for breakfast, unless you write cookbooks, or your fiction includes cooking as part of the theme, or it's part of your *personal side* of being a writer. Bob talks constantly about his dogs Cool

Gus and Sassy Becca. Here they are during his drive across the country.

Bob will Tweet a lot about his dogs. It gives readers a glimpse into him as a person, without getting too personal. This helps break up the Tweets about all his great books. Tweeting links to your blog posts is a great way to attract readers.

A great community building technique is to Tweet about other people's blog posts. If you come across a blog that you really love, you don't have to know the person to Tweet a link and say *hey, check out this great blog post by so and so.* A caveat here. Don't just constantly RT your friends and favorite people. Be genuine and kind. If you love the post, let your followers know. If you don't, no need to forward it on.

You can also start conversations. One thing Bob used to do was to Tweet famous lines from movies. His followers had fun either Tweeting back lines from the same movie or trying to guess which movie his lines were from. They even tried to stump Bob on movie quotes.

You can also create your own hashtag. We've seen many authors do this for their books, characters, or just for support with other writers. Remember that any hashtag you create is public and open to the public. You can respectfully ask others not to promote their blogs or put buy links for their books, but you can't really "force" the rule. We have found that most are respectful of the hashtag rules, but only when the ones who created it consistently post on the hashtag and gently remind others of the rules.

Other hashtags that have been created are ones like #writegoal, #pubit, #wewrite and #amwriting, all geared toward writers and a great way to find new people to follow. Also, it's a great way to network when conferences are happening.

We also see reader hashtags such as #fridayreads and #amreading. These tags might be useful for authors to comment on and also give recommendations for their favorite authors. It is one way to make connections with your readers without overtly promoting your book.

When Bob was at Digital Book World (#DBW12) he used the hashtag to tweet interesting facts he learned. People attending his panel tweeted quotes from him and other authors, giving those not able to attend a chance to following along while it was happening.

Jen did not attend the conference, but she followed the tweets and by doing so made a connection with a fellow technology buff who gave Jen some interesting insight into a program Jen was considering buying to help with the technical side of the business.

It is perfectly fine to announce your book release and Twitter buy links. It's also perfectly acceptable to do it regularly, as long as it's not all you do.

Many people will link their tweets to their Facebook page and other social media sites. We find this can be effective, but it can also be annoying and some might consider it a sign of laziness, or worse, a sign of not caring. One of the things we do is use Network blogs. This sends out our blog posts over a network. We also link WordPress to Facebook and Twitter, but we also have conversations with people on each site.

If you are new to Twitter and want to know who to follow, go to twitter.com/Bob_Mayer and twitter.com/jentalty and check out who is following us and who we are following and then pick and choose who you wish to follow.

Again, the key here is consistency and communication.

Facebook

Facebook has groups and chats and all sorts of things writers and readers can use to connect with each other. It's an excellent tool and we believe it can be very effective, if you work it; but it's time consuming and requires you to focus on it and, once more, consistency is key.

It's always good to start out small and build slowly, so take your time in finding "friends." Start your page and then decide how personal or professional you want to make it. Remember, social media is a tool and the key element that makes it work is that it is *social*. You must interact with people. Same with Twitter, it can't be all "buy my book."

We've found groups that focus on independent publishing, self-publishing, critique groups and other writing groups on Facebook. These groups usually allow people to post links and start conversations. You will get out of it what you put in to it. That is true with any social media site.

We created a Write It Forward group for those people who have taken one of our Write It Forward workshops where they can continue to engage and network with fellow classmates.

Take the time to figure out what you want to say about yourself. Have a short bio that covers all your platforms. Upload your covers to the image section and make albums. Jen has been known to upload covers she's working on, showing the various steps and different designs she comes up with until she lands on the perfect cover.

Make sure when you join or are invited into these groups that you are respective of their rules. While we are firm believers in knowing the rules and breaking the rules with good reason, it is important to be respectful. Some groups are more supportive and don't want anyone promoting their blog or buy links to their books. The truth is, the more you engage people, the more likely they are to go find your books without you telling them to. Every time you comment, you are leaving a link back to your Facebook page, where you will have images and information about how you are and what you do.

Facebook also uses the 'like' system, which used to be known as Fan Pages. Many authors use fan pages and keep their personal pages to family and close personal friends.

Kindleboards and other boards

Kindleboards (http://kindleboards.com) is a great place for authors who have published their books on Kindle. Why? Because Kindle owners hang out there. And, you can discuss strategies with other authors who are in the trenches and learn from those actually self-publishing.

Kindleboards has a variety of discussions that range from talk about the new Kindle Fire, Accessories, Reader discussions, Book Clubs, Reviews, Writing Cafe and even a Not Quite Kindle topic.

Before venturing on to the boards, take some time to read over the rules. There are places you can promote, and places you can't, and for very good reasons. One thing that Kindleboards does that we love, is giving you the option to create a signature line that has your book covers and links to Amazon where everyone can purchase your books. That means that when you are posting anywhere on the board, your signature line shows up. Automatic promotion without it being intrusive.

There are also rules about how often you can post on your own promotion thread in the Book Bazaar. Here is a spreadsheet that Bob uses to keep track of all his books on the Kindleboards, the UK Kindleboards and on the Nookboards.

Book	photo	Kindle link	date	next bump	UK Kindle link	date	next bump	Nook link	date	next bump
Area 51	http://i1104.p	http://www.	12/25	1/1	http://www.	12/25	1/1	http://www.	12/25	1/1
Bermuda Tri	http://i1104.p	http://www.	12/25	1/1	http://www.	12/25	1/1	http://www.	12/25	1/1
Synbat	http://i1104.p	http://www.	12/25	1/1	http://www.	12/25	1/1	http://www.	12/25	1/1
Jefferson	http://i1104.p	http://www.	12/25	1/1	http://www.	12/25	1/1	http://www.	12/25	1/1
Lost Girls	http://i1104.p	http://www.	12/25	1/1	http://www.	12/25	1/1	http://www.	12/25	1/1

This helps Bob stay organized and 'bump' his threads on the correct date (they allow you to bump a promo thread every seven days on all the boards in the appropriate forum). They are very strict about promotion. They have to be, otherwise the entire board would be one big advertisement.

Since Bob has so many books, he bumps five to seven titles every day. While we're not sure how effective that is regarding sales, a key psychological point is that keeping a regular schedule for bumping the threads keeps his focus on promoting. At one point he went over six months without missing a single day of bumping his threads, until one day he was traveling and didn't have access to the Internet. Looking at the dates of the bumps, gives an indication of consistency. Or lack thereof. Thus, some of the things you do might not have direct benefits, but don't discount the indirect ones.

There are also many great discussions on the boards about publishing, cover art, where to find the best cover artists (though Who

Dares Wins Publishing snatched up the best with Jen!) and anything else you might want to know about digital publishing.

There are many other boards for writers, and once again it comes down to which boards you enjoy, feel comfortable on and which meet your needs as an author. The key is to be consistent.

There are many other social media sites, and we don't pretend to know them all or what works best. These are the sites we use the most. We do also use Goodreads, which we hear great things about from other authors and will be exploring in 2012.

The key to social media is it should be fun and effective. If you break out in hives every time you open your social media site, it's time to try something different or use Write It Forward techniques to venture out of your comfort zone into your courage zone.

You also must be patient when using social media. Expecting results the moment you enter the scene is the kiss of death. You've Twittered, Facebooked, blogged, Goodreads, and utilized other social media outlets and today you sold one book, so it must not work. Or, you've been consistent for a month, and still, sales are slow, it must not work.

Writers tend to be impatient. We demand results from ourselves, so we expect it elsewhere, especially when we've put in the time. But have we waited to see the "real" result before switching gears? The number one thing we finally came up with regard to promoting that eventually worked was to be consistent. To pick where and how to spend our time and energy, and then to do it every single day, regardless of what results we were getting. There is a tipping point, an almost magical point where things start to work. The problem is you don't know where that point is. But if you quit, you'll never reach it.

Using Social Media Effectively

Bob's a guy, and like any guy, he thinks in terms of dollar signs. Jen does too, but she goes beyond the dollar sign and looks at what our promotional efforts are really generating.

There is a book called **What Sticks** by Rex Briggs and Greg Stuart. They state an advertising truth that is universal: "I know half my advertising is wasted — I just don't know which half." They also go on to say that they believe you can figure out which half is wasted if you put in the effort. We put in the effort and found we were using social media ineffectively for both our time and money.

It's almost impossible to track sales when the majority of our sales are from places like Amazon and B&N. They track buying behavior, but they don't share it with us and even then, unless you have a reader explaining why they bought your book, it's impossible to track where they came from. Was it Twitter? Facebook? A friend? By accident? We don't know, so we have to stop looking at whether or not social media sold anything; it's helping to create good will and a social media professional following, which will lead to word of mouth. "Hey, did you happen to read so and so's blog? They recommended this book and everyone is raving about it."

Using Google Alert, we go to any blog or site that mentions anything about us and we thank whoever wrote it, and, if appropriate, contribute to the conversation. We also use statistical information from WordPress that tells us where people are clicking into our site from and any pingbacks. It's important to be aware of who your visitors are and where they are coming form. A great way to build connections is to go to other people's blogs and post intelligent comments relating to the topic. People read the comments on their own blogs. This brings you to their attention.

Social media helps build your presence, create a community, and develop personal and professional relationships...all of which leads to the number one way to sell a book...word of mouth.

Social Media Bottom Line

The key to social media and networking is to build community. You have to push your emphasis on building your brand and contacts rather than selling books. Sales come out of laying the groundwork.

Social media, while it plays a large part in a writer's life, is just one of many tools. If you are consistent in your social media, consistent in your message and are genuine, your efforts, over time, will begin to pay off.

MARKETING STRATEGIES

If I build it, they will come....

As writers, we have to hook our readers in the first few pages. As marketers we have to hook potential readers to visit our cover and product description so they can get to the hook in the first few pages.

Writers are usually not the best Promoters or Sellers. We're writers. So, this part of the job is usually not in our comfort zone. Also, many of us don't know how to develop a good marketing plan. The best advice is to watch, listen and learn from the authors doing it in both the traditionally published world and the self-publishing world.

Learn how places like Kindle at Amazon works. There are things we found such as how important it is to get in the top #100 of any given category.

Marketing and the Writer

Often Marketing, Promotion and Sales get tossed around as if they are the same thing. They are not. There is a very good reason why the Marketing Department and the Sales Department are separate. Promotion is a part of marketing, but not all of marketing.

It's important for a writer to understand how all this plays into their career, especially in the current marketplace. It doesn't matter if you are traditionally published or self-published; you're going to need a marketing plan. Understanding the basics is key to success.

Marketing is a set of activities and a process for creating and communicating something that will have value for customers. Marketing is a Strategy. It's the plan. It's the initial shift from creating a product to getting the product out there.

Sales is the act of selling a product or service in return for money or some other type of compensation.

The relationship between marketing and sales is important because while they are different, they have the same goal. Marketing improves the selling environment. Marketing is used to increase the number of interactions between product and consumer. Promotional efforts are used to help bring customers in.

Promotion is inside of marketing. It is one of the four elements in the marketing mix.

There is an argument that Marketing can potentially negate the need for sales. It's the idea that once great marketing and solid promotion are set in place it will bring more people "through the door." Social Media is a great tool if used properly to build a community of people "walking through the door." It's important to mention your books and what you write on social media, but avoid the "buy me" syndrome.

Marketing in the past often included Advertising and it was seen as the creative side of business, but the academic study of science, (which uses social sciences, psychology, sociology, math, and other sciences) makes Marketing now widely recognized as a science. Many colleges offer Marketing Master of Science (MSc) programs.

This history of Marketing is actually quite fascinating. Up until the 1950s, we were production-oriented when it came to driving profit. This was based on the idea that consumer tastes would not rapidly change.

Through the 1960s, we were Product-oriented when it came to driving profit. The idea here was that as long as the product was good, it would sell, but also during this time we became sales-oriented. Remember the door-to-door salesman? This was actually selling the product you already have to the consumer.

But from the 1970s to today, the orientation of business switched to a Marketing base when it comes to driving profit. The idea is to base marketing plans around marketing concepts and supply the products that will satisfy new consumer tastes. Companies began researching consumer wants and desires and then used R&D to develop a product that would satisfy those desires. Find out what they want and then get it to them before the competition does.

What does this have to do with being an author? Marketing is a strategy. It's a plan. The field of Marketing encompasses everything a company does (writer/publisher) in the management of any given product (book). The biggest part of your marketing plan is WRITING YOUR BOOK.

When it comes to books content is king. PRODUCT rules. Your book has to be good to succeed long-term AND it has to be something the public desires (and we all know how fickle consumers can be when it comes to books). The good news is that no matter what you are writing...there is a market for it...but you have to understand the consumers in that given market and find your niche. Niche is key to succeeding in publishing on the Internet.

Being a writer is a catch-22 sometimes. We hear all the time "don't write to the market." Yet, we hear all the time from editors and agents, "I can't sell that. Give me something I can sell in the current market."

We post on Write It Forward, and will continue to post, information on the craft of writing. Your quality book is the foundation for any marketing plan. Writing the better book is the most important aspect of being a writer. Your marketing plan will come out of that.

There are many variables to consider when developing your Marketing Plan as a writer. The plan has to fit with your overall career goals.

You can market your book, but you can't sell your book. The only book we've ever seen being successfully "sold" by selling methods is the Encyclopedia.

When should a writer begin to Market their book?

The question really should be *when should a writer begin to market themselves?* There are a million opinions on this subject found all over the web and at various writer conferences. We are of the opinion that there is no time like the present, but never at the expense of learning and honing your craft. You should not wait until your book is published since it's not about sales but building brand.

We see a lot of writers on various social media sites sending out blog links on various topics and working toward building community and readership. This is good, especially if you have a strong non-fiction platform. Bob's post on the killing of Bin Laden was one of our most popular blogs. This was the case for two reasons:

Hot Topic at the time
And Bob is a former Green Beret (expert in the field of Special Operations)

Another very popular blog post was our post "indie" vs. "trad,"regarding the rift between traditional published authors and independent published authors. Again, for two reasons:

Hot Topic
We've done both successfully

So what is it you want to say to the world and why?
And why should people listen?
We mentioned presence marketing. The more people see your name associated with "something," the larger the presence. Writers on social media who are not currently published (either traditionally or independently) are building communities and relationships often with other writers. This is a great way be involved in the writing community and your name is being associated with "writing."

The problem with jumping in to the wonderful world of promotion too soon, is not knowing yourself as a writer. Unless you have a strong platform in something writers/readers would be interested in (cop, medical examiner, lawyer, mass murderer...) it's hard to build platform. Also, as we grow and develop our craft, who we are as writers changes.

The key to promotion and marketing before publishing is connection and networking. Going to conferences, being on social media and "talking" to other people who share a common interest. Don't get too worked up about needing to have a "thing." Be yourself. When Jen developed her first blog back in 2003, it was titled: "The Queen of Darkness." She blogged about her research into the darker side of human nature, wrote reviews of dark books and movies, and interviewed authors. She focused on her interests. After she published, she changed the focus. When she began teaching, she shifted focus again, finally settling on a blended approach as we both blog about the craft of writing as much as we do about the business based on our collective 30+ years in this business. One thing to remember is that the more niche you get, the easier it is to find your specific readers. Too often writers are great at building community with other writers, but finding the reader is a much more difficult process.

Much of this happens organically as you take baby-steps in social media, but always remember the writing has to come first. Spend most of your time writing a better book.

The next question then becomes what does a writer do after they either make the sale to a traditional publisher or decide to self-publish? Should I have a dedicated blog for the book? Fan page for the book? Postcards? Newsletters? Business cards? Book trailers? Where do I begin?

The key is to have a one-year marketing plan and re-evaluate what you are doing every six months and where you *feel* your efforts are making the most impact. We say feel because much of your promotional efforts cannot be measured. Once more, the key is consistency. Once you determine what you want to do, you have to keep doing it, often in the face of seeing little in the way of results.

A caveat. What works for one may not work for another. Just like writing, there is no one way to promote a book. The key to success is to look around at what everyone else is doing and assess if doing that is something you *can* do and something that makes sense to you.

Paper Products and Promotion

Bookmarks seem to be a rite of passage for an author, although it's one we've never invested in. Why? Because there was a fundamental disconnect between a bookmark and an eBook release.

That isn't to say we don't think they have value. Anything with your name, contact information and book information on it has value. However, we think there are better uses of paper promotion. How many times have you bought a book because of a bookmark? At many conferences, tables are crammed with similar looking bookmarks and few are ever picked up.

Business Cards are gateways to your web site. The brochure is almost outdated, although we do use them at times. Your website is your brochure. Your business card is a way for people to find it. It's also a way for people to contact you via email. We believe you should always have contact information on your website, but some people don't want people to be able to do that, so it's essential to get their business card.

When we get a business card from someone we've spoken to, the first chance we get, we write down quick notes about the contact on the back. Notes like what was discussed, and what to follow up on.

Postcards. We use postcards. Not to mail, although anytime anyone purchases a book from Who Dares Wins Publishing we send along a post card about an upcoming release, offer a special discount and information on our workshops, along with a brochure and one of our business cards.

But the question is how effective are they? We are not sure they are, but we still do them. Why? Presence marking. It all comes back to presence marketing. When Jen is at a conference she goes looking for three things in the goodie room:

Pens
Post-it notes
Unusual and unique marketing tools

Pens and post-it notes are useful. Jen has a ton of pens with her name on them and she is always trying to convince Bob to get some for himself. We don't think they sell books, but Jen goes looking for Hannah Howell Pens and Post-it notes at every conference. Why? Hannah has the best purple pens ever and the post-it notes are great. Jen uses them when she's reading/researching using non-fiction books or when she is deconstructing a novel for structure.

The problem with giving away pens and post-it notes is that EVERYONE is doing them. How will yours stand out and be unique?

The most creative physical promotional product we have even seen was done by Sarah Grimm at RWA Nationals in Atlanta. Her book title was *Not Without Risk* and it was a Romantic Suspense novel. The title played off two aspects, the suspense and the sex...let's just say the condom broke in the book. Sarah had printed up labels with *Not Without Risk by Sarah Grimm* and stuck them with a couple hundred red condoms. She became known as "the condom lady." Did it sell books? Maybe a few, but the promotional efforts were effective because people are still talking about it, especially now as the book has been re-released.

The key with physical product promotional items is to make sure they fit either your book, or your overall platform. These are not items you need to spend a lot of money on. Places like Vista Print and National Pen are wonderful for such items. What we like about Vista Print is that they have so many "free" things that the only thing you end up paying for is either a design upload charge or printing. We'll generally get a couple hundred business cards for the cost of postage.

The bottom line is these items are tools and can be effective in building name recognition, but you have to get them out there in order for them to be effective.

Paid Advertising and PR Programs

It's always been Bob's mantra that you can't market fiction, but you have to market fiction...but you can't.   Why do you have to? Because no one else will do it for you. The key is that whether you self-publish or get traditionally published, you have to do the same things to market your work.   Unless you get at least a six figure advance from a major publisher, their marketing campaign for your book will be minimal.

Paid Advertising

Every couple of months we get an email for *Romance Sells*. It's a magazine that goes to libraries and booksellers. A lot of authors who are not with a publisher place ads in the magazine themselves. It costs a couple hundred dollars. We chose not to do this. It is highly unlikely that any bookseller or library is going to pick up a POD or eBook, although this will change as libraries go digital and on-line. This ties in to understanding your product and who will be buying it.

Jen also gets a variety of emails about placement ads in *Romantic Times*, both through her previous publisher, The Wild Rose Press, and an author who puts together group ads for authors. The key with *Romantic Times* is that some books that have paid placement will get a review.

You can buy space in the *RWR*, which is Romance Writer's of America's publication. You can buy space in other magazines. How effective are they? It depends on how often your advertisement is going to be seen by the same person in other formats. It also depends on is the strength of the ad. What makes the ad unique? What kind of emotion will it invoke in the receiver? For the average author who is putting their own time and money into paid advertising, it's probably not the most effective way to get the news out about your book. New York Publishers do paid advertising but it's often a way to make the big name author feel better rather than for sales.

Facebook, Google, Goodreads, LinkedIn and other social media ads

Presence marketing--the more people see your name, your book covers, read and hear your creed, the more likely they are to remember you. Ads like these are not about instant purchases. They are about building name recognition. Also, if readers constantly see your name and covers in various places and then come across a book by you when they are "searching" for something to read, they are more likely to buy because they recognize the name, even if they don't know where they recognize it from.

We have these types of ads running for all our authors. We rotate out different covers and feature each author. You set your cost limit per day, run your ad for a set time (or not) and you pay either per click or per impressions.

The key to deciding which way to go is based on a couple of factors.

- Are you using the ad to build your on-line Internet presence and brand?
- Are you trying to drive traffic to your site? Your Fan Page?
- Are you trying to sell a specific product from a specific site?

Also, you need to look at what your CTR of your ad will be. What is CTR? CTR is your Click Through Rate and it is the percentage rate at which people click on your ad. So, if you ad is seen by 100 people but only one person clicked on it, then your CTR is 1%. FYI, I lost Bob at hello.

The question is which way, CPM or CPC is the most cost effective? This all depends on the CTR percentage. The higher the CTR, the lower the cost per click. If you have a low CTR, you are better going with pay per impressions because those clicks will cost you less. Follow?

How do you find out? When you fill out the information for your ad for the very first time, the CTR will be estimated. Once your ad has run for a short period of time, the CTR will be calculated and you will have a better idea of how many times customers are actually clicking on your ad.

We recommend going with a CPM ad to start with for at least a full month. What is great is you can set a lifetime budget or a daily budget. We use a daily budget and adjust each month according to our ad needs and current advertising budget. This way we can feature new releases, free promotions and specials we have on our website. We have at least 10 different ads going on at any given time for all of our authors.

Your budget, depending on the venue can be as low as a $1.00 per day (would need to be CPM) or as high as $100.00 a day or higher. You could set a "lifetime" budget, meaning once you hit say $500.00 for your ad, the ad ends.

The argument we've hard for going with CPC is you ONLY pay per click, where with CPM you are paying just to have your ad seen. My marketing background dictates that ad seen is an impression of Bob Mayer, Duty, Honor, Country on your brain. Each time we impress that on your brain we increase our changes of you buying the book…. if you click, it's icing on the cake.

Running ads through Impressions over Clicks is the better marketing plan for most authors. It's all about building a presence and getting your name, your book, in front of your readers.

We can't measure the effectiveness or if these ads result in sales, but for the time and cost we put into them and the fact they have the potential of reaching millions of people, they are well worth it since our short-term goal is not to sell, but to increase our presence marketing. The more people see Write It Forward workshops, and the more times they see it, the more likely they are to tell their writer friends about the workshops and/or sign up.

We might get only sixteen clicks on the ad, but it pops up 250,000 times on the edge of the page. We view this as subconsciously marketing the book cover and title.

PR Plans

There are a lot of PR agencies for Authors. Their goal is to increase your presence marketing and increase your sales. They help you create an image, find opportunities in marketing and promotion, media exposure and try to get you the most effective marketing money can buy. Many of these firms are now focusing on the Internet. Consultants are popping up all over the place to set up your social media platform. The reality is that most are selling a boilerplate program. To get a publicity campaign built specifically for you, your brand, and your book, is very costly.

One of the things we did with the release of *Duty, Honor, Country*, was have one of our authors who worked in PR for decades (Victoria Martínez) write an excellent press release that we sent out to a variety of media sources. We also paid for an ad with WebPR, an online source that will get you both national media coverage and local coverage. Our ad was picked up by publications such as the *Boston Globe*, the *New Yorker* and a couple dozen others. The key is to use the right key words in the title and one word description, something we learned from Victoria. This cost a little over $300.

We also used our email list/newsletter to announce the release of the book. We did a blog post. We also created a blog dedicated to West Point and the Civil War. Bob shot a podcast and loaded it to YouTube. We used all our social media resources.

When DHC was released, it hit a couple top 100 categories on Amazon. Was it Bob's good name and reputation? The Press Release? The email announcement? Social Media? We honestly have no idea, but for the time and money we put into the release campaign, it was worth it.

In general, we're leery of PR firms for fiction authors. The first thing a good PR person will ask you is: Who is your market? Who is the consumer of your product? Because they have to target that market. But for fiction, it's very, very hard to get an idea of who exactly your market is. Every novel is a unique commodity. Non-fiction is a different matter. There, you can target an audience and get specific and a PR firm might be well worth it. For fiction, unless you have a really unique hook that has news appeal, it's much more difficult.

If you have a traditional publisher behind you, you've got their marketing, sales, and PR departments behind you. However, remember they are focused on getting orders from distributors. You will still need to market yourself and your books and connect with your readers.

The bottom line is to find those things that you can do, that don't cost a lot of money, but will get your name and your books in front of potential readers. The key is being consistent in your time and efforts.

Social Media and Blogging

We talked about social media and blogging and all the various types and platforms available to the writer. It should be viewed as a portion of your overall marketing strategy. It's a great way to keep your name out there and it's something you can always do. So is blogging. We try to blog two to three times a week. The key with all of it is to reciprocate. Go to other blogs and comment. Don't do it for the sake of doing it, but do it when you have something to add to the conversation. Visit those who visit your blog. Comment on blogs you like to read. Don't promote, but link back to your blog by signing in when you comment.

You have to make a commitment to blogging if you are going to do it. You must entertain and inform. You must post at least once a week. We see a drop off in hits after three days on any blog post.

One thing you can do if you have a nonfiction topic you are an expert in, is use your blog to literally write a nonfiction book, blog post by blog post. This way you are achieving two things simultaneously.

We do not recommend posting excerpts from novels either on a blog or online. We don't feel they are effective. In the same way, we tried serializing a novel in eBook, thinking we might harken back to the days of Dickens. It didn't work. People want the entire book right away, not in pieces.

THE PRICING OF EBOOKS AND PERCEIVED VALUE

The explosion of eBooks and the number of midlist and new authors choosing to self-publish has brought about some heated discussions on price point and perceived value. How much should we charge for an eBook? 0.99? $2.99? $6.99? $9.99? $14.99? What is too much? What is not enough?

Many authors are upset over the $0.99 eBook. They argue that it's devaluing the work of the writer. That it somehow tells potential readers that the writer and their work is only worth $0.99. We understand the argument. We know what it takes to write a book, and our time is worth far more than $0.99 for the year it took to write.

However, if we sold 1,500 copies in one month of that one book (which we have done this month on several venues) then the book is worth 1,500 x .99 x .35 = $519.70. That is number of books multiplied by price of books multiplied by royalty given by Amazon/PubIt = total income for one month. It's not an earth shattering number, but that is only one book out of many books we offer, most of which we are charging $2.99 to $4.99 for and getting 70% royalty rate. We have only a few books at $0.99 and they are leads to series or genres, such as the first **Atlantis** book, and **Eyes of the Hammer**, which was Bob's first thriller ever published.

Price point is a marketing tool, and when considering price, a business owner must evaluate the range for what consumers are willing to pay (and it doesn't have to do with the value of the writers' time or the value of a single book). The idea behind the bargain book is to pull readers in, hook them on the quality product so they will buy other books (at the higher, and valued, price).

When we write a book, we need to get into the minds of the reader or we end up with too much backstory, or too much over explaining, or give the reader information they don't need. When we enter the business of publishing we have to do the same thing, and stop thinking like a writer and think like a consumer and a business person and, most important, the customer.

Readers do troll for the $0.99 eBook. We can tell that by looking at sales figures. If they don't like the book, there is no great loss. They don't buy from the author again, but if they did like what they read, they gobble up everything they can find from that author...and at regular prices.

There is another argument about how eBooks should be the same price or close to a paperback book because the content of the book is the same. The theory is that just because it costs less to produce the eBook doesn't mean the content is any different; therefore it is worth the same price. Then wouldn't that be true for the hardcover and the paperback? Identical content. Consumers wait all the time for the book to come out in paperback because they refuse to pay the higher price for the same product. Additionally, let's consider a $6.99 paperback for which the author is receiving an 8% royalty from the publisher. That means the author gets $0.56 per book sold. For a $2.99 eBook, the self-published author gets a 70% royalty from the distributor, minus some other minor charges, but it comes out to $1.99. So, the $2.99 eBook make the author almost four times the royalty of the print book.

But we'll tell you what makes absolutely no sense. Pricing an eBook between $10 and $19.98, where, strangely, many traditionally published eBooks are priced. Here's why it doesn't make sense: go below $2.99 or above $9.99, your royalty rate goes from 70% to 35%. Therefore, any eBook over $9.99, up until it hits $19.98, is actually making *less* money than an eBook priced at $9.99. Traditional publishers are sticking with higher prices for eBooks for several reasons, but a major one is the Agency Pricing model where they get to set prices in exchange for a fixed royalty rate from the platform.

Instead of being concerned about the $0.99 eBook, authors need to really be concerned about the blatantly destructive agency pricing models many publishers are using. A big advantage the self-published author has over the traditionally published author is control over pricing.

One of the reasons the price has been driven down is because of the influx of books being put out on the web. This is partially related to the law of supply and demand. But another reason the price is being driven down is due to another P in the marketing mix: Placement.

You can't sell your book if your product isn't seen. In traditional publishing that meant the racks at the front of the store. Indie Authors are getting their placement via a lower pricing strategy.

We've discovered a key to 'placement' for eBooks is to get on a bestseller list in a specific genre. Amazon breaks books down to subgenres and lists the top 100. For example, *Atlantis*, is now in the top 50 overall on UK Kindle sales, and has been as high as #2 in science fiction, just behind *Game of Thrones*. It's in the top 10 in science fiction in the US, nestled among, again, all the *Game of Thrones* books. **Chasing The Ghost** started as a $0.99 book, hooked a place in the top ten in men's adventure, we raised the price to $2.99, and it's still there in the top 10. Why? Because it's a good book. But we needed that $0.99 lead to get it that 'placement'.

'Free' is another marketing tool. With Amazon KDP Select, you go exclusive with Amazon for three months and in that time, get to list your book for free for five days. It appears it can be a very effective marketing tool. We just tried Kindle Select, and while the results aren't all in, the key is the ability to list a book for free for five days during the three months it's exclusive on Amazon and can be borrowed. The down side to the program is the exclusivity. It means the book must be pulled from all other eBook retail sites. The upside is that giving it away for free can really help.

On Bob's *Atlantis*, we had around 24,000 free downloads in five day. Since then, the book went for sale and was ranked at 37,866. You lose all your previous ranking which isn't good. But since then, the book has steadily climbed and after just three days is currently #232 overall on Kindle, and #4 in science fiction, which is definitely good. Thus, we feel it's a worthwhile program and are going to rotate a number of titles through the program over the course of the year. We're not going to leave any title in the program more than the required three months.

Publishing has changed a lot, but it's still a business. Part of our job is to understand that business. There needs to be a balance. We can't promote or price a product if we haven't taken the time to better our craft. But, on the other hand, if we don't take the time to understand what is happening in the business, we reduce our chances of selling our books to our readers.

Price point is a tool. One that can be abused. But it is one that can send you to the top of the Amazon lists and earn you a nice royalty check at the end of the month. We have to use the tools in our marketing plan effectively and wait to see if they work. It's not instant gratification, even though we can see the results daily; it takes time for all this to meld together. For any price change, you need at least two months of results to tell if it is making any difference.

Product Placement

This has been frustrating for us as indie authors. But it was frustrating for Bob when he was in traditional publishing, as placement in the brick and mortar store went to those few, select titles the publisher was willing to back with co-op money. Amazon doesn't offer any paid placement. Barnes and Noble on the other hand have started a new program which launched this week for indie authors, and Bob was the first author to be part of the program called "Nook First." (Actually, the program was Bob's idea.) In this program you publish your book exclusively to Nook for one month in return for promotion and placement.

Amazon has Amazon Select, which launched in December 2011. We discussed it earlier. Select has been a hot topic among authors and this is indicative of the state of publishing affairs today. There are often heated arguments about the "right" way to do things. We don't believe there is one blanket answer for everyone. What works for some people, doesn't work for others. That's why you have to carefully sift through all the information that is being disseminated. One thing to always check is the platform of the person behind the information. Are they an author? An agent? A publisher? One of the many self-appointed gurus of publishing? What agenda are they pursuing? Is it the same as your agenda?

A key is to take your emotions out of it and try to subjectively evaluate things. Remember, something you think makes no sense to do today, might be just the thing you are embracing a few months from now. Also, you are going to have to chances. If you play it safe, you might not have a large failure but you also won't have any great successes.

Luck

144

The first book in the *Area 51* series was listed as a new release on PubIt the week it came out. This was not anything we did. We got lucky. Then the book hit their scifi bestseller lists and then was also in the top 50 of all books sold on Nook. Week after week, our book cover was on the best of scifi on the homepage of the Nook. Of course, when B&N "lost" the book, we lost our placement. And sales have declined because of it. Luck, though, tends to go to people who have . . .

Hard work and perseverance

When we released *The Jefferson Allegiance*, we contacted a blogger that recommends Nook Books. Since it was a one-month exclusive with B&N, we contacted a blogger that recommends Nook books. Between the blog and a little promotion from Barnes and Noble, *The Jefferson Allegiance* soared to #2 nationally on Nook.

The key is we are never done. We are constantly looking at ways to help promote all our books. We look into every promotional possibility. We don't do them all, but we look at what they offer and then decide if it is in our budget and if it will fit in our over all plan.

You have to market yourself. You've built it. Now invite the readers in.

Metadata/SEO/Analytics

Readers Rule!

The most important person for an author to get to know is their reader. When a person reads one of your books for the first time, they are getting to know how you write and how that is going to make them feel. You are making a promise to that reader for the next book.

There are two different types of readers: The printed book reader and the digital book reader. While these two different readers are blending together to one common marketplace, we are not totally there yet. How the author communicates with the each type of reader is a little different. Both the print reader and the digital reader first go by word of mouth. When it comes to purchasing products, we rely heavily on our peers for recommendations. But the digital reader can be reached in ways the print reader cannot, and as this market grows so does the ability to be discovered by these readers. The digital reader can search for you, but can only find you if you have done the work of making your metadata the most accessible.

KNOWING THE EBOOK MARKET, METADATA AND DISCOVERABILITY

Some statistics that were given at the Publishers Launch Conference:
In May 2009, the eBook market was only about 3% of all readership. In October 2010, it was about 5% of total readership. In February 2011, it grew to 15%. In August 2011, it grew to 16%. Also, the US market is paying for 57% of digital downloads. In the US, it was reported that 64% of eBook buyers are women. 33% of eBook buyers are between the ages of 30 and 44. 19% of eBook buyers are over the age of 65. The next largest group is 55-64 at 17%, and 18-29 is only 12%, and the 13-17 they report 0%. Why is this important? Each age group has a "trigger" that drives their purchases.

Then there are the reasons for buying eBooks. There are 7 influencers.

7. Recommendation from an eBook store sent over email--about 37%
6. Seeing the title on a bestseller list--about 38%
5. Receiving a free/promotional eBook by same author--about 39%
4. Reading a print book review--about 40%
3. Seeing a low price in an advertisement--about 41%
2. Reading an online book review--about 42%
1. Receiving a free/promotional sample chapter--about 43%

The next question that comes to mind is: How do the eBook buyers become aware of authors and their titles? About 30% of readers become aware when they receive a free/promotional chapter. About the same percentage from reading a print review. About 33% of readers find out about titles from bestseller lists, and roughly the same percentage from seeing a low price somewhere, and finally 36% from reading an online book review.

Take all those statistics with a grain of salt. They are based on information that is coming faster than most market research people can up with. However, by knowing the 7 key influencers and how readers become aware of any given eBook, you can begin to plan your marketing strategies to hit your target audience by use of metadata such as reviews, bestseller mentions, etc. Add basic metadata such as title, author, and publisher to enhanced metadata like covers and author biography, which give potential customers enough opportunity to be drawn in and decide that your book is the book for them.

Unique Identity

Better known as an ISBN.

We hear all the time how it is not necessary to have an ISBN. You don't need one to upload to Amazon or to B&N. Why? They assign their own identifiers unique to their system. This is a good and bad thing. If you are only selling on those platforms and don't care about crossover, then you're fine, but understand that the rest of the publishing industry uses ISBNs to track sales. Also, having one identifier such as an ISBN increases that lovely word that Bob loves to use these days "discoverability.". As a publisher, when we communicate to distributors, it is by ISBN, especially when it comes to distributing eBooks through Lightning Source, uploading to Kobo and also to iBooks. When we receive special orders from bookstores for some of our books they do so by requesting using a specific ISBN. Thus we recommend getting an ISBN for your book.

What is Metadata?

The definition of metadata is simply the set of data which describes and gives information about other data or data about data. Metadata helps describe, explain and locate information in a machine understandable form. Metadata can be stored (your product description, price, etc.) or it can be embedded as a digital object (links to outside sources and in the case of books, the text in the book).

Metadata helps facilitate discovery of relevant material. It brings similar material together and it distinguishes dissimilar resources.

Metadata needs to be visible across multiple platforms. It isn't just about the book, but about you as an author. You as a brand.

At the very basic fundamental level, metadata (outside of title and author) are the categories you place your book in. Barnes and Noble, Kindle, Smashwords and even iBooks make this process pretty simple. We discussed it in the digital process where we went over how many categories you can have your book listed in. However, if you go through other sources, like direct upload to Kobo, you will need to use BISG, which promotes book industry standards for labeling print, and digital discovery identifiers. Both iBooks and Kobo give authors the options to upload via industry-approved data carrier formats like ONIX, which uses BISG categories. This ensures your book is in the best possible category so that during searches readers can "discover" you.

Side note: When we upload to Kobo we use a special spreadsheet provided by Kobo that uses the BISG categories. This spreadsheet can also be used for iBooks. It makes sure all your data is the same across all platforms making you more discoverable.

Check out BISG at www.bisg.org for more information on the most common standards and best practices. They also have information on the ONIX system.

Going beyond Identifiers

Once you have the basic (author, title, price, etc.) and enhanced (product description, cover, etc.) metadata in place, it's time to take metadata to the next level. Many retailers index basic book content. When you index the content you increase discoverability. The "Search Inside the Book" feature at Amazon helps increase discoverability because their system will pick up on keywords, phrases, time, setting and place, and assigns relevancy to each keyword during customer searches. So, if you are writing about Area 51 and Aliens and how Bob Mayer has been abducted seventeen times and has the blueprints for the mother ship, you want to make sure the key words are in the description, in the keywords, in the tags you use, and anywhere else you can think.

Another thing to consider when dealing with metadata is the source document itself. With digital files we deal with everything in the text whether it is the words on the page, the HTML coding, or whatever source code is being used, which creates metadata. This is in part why Jen is a stickler for clean code.

The bottom line is you want your book to be found on every site it's listed and in all search engines by keywords that your readers will use.

Search Engine Optimizer (SEO)

SEO is the process of improving visibility of a website or a web page in a specific search. While SEO and Metadata are not the same thing, they are linked. Metadata is specific to the sites that are going to carry your books and when you choose wording for product description, etc., you need to think in terms of "customer searches."

SEO is a much broader scope because you've moved from specific sites such as Amazon or Barnes and Noble to the entire Internet.

Exercise: Go Google your NAME, BOOK TITLE, BLOG NAME and anything else you can think of when it comes to your brand.

Bob Mayer and Jen Talty

When we Google Bob's name this is the first page.

Google

bob mayer

Search

About 24,700,000 results (0.29 seconds)

Everything
Images
Maps
Videos
News
Shopping
Books
More

East Rochester, NY

Change location

All results
Sites with images
More search tools

Bob Mayer Home Page
www.bobmayer.org/
Bob Mayer's Home Page. What can I do for you based on my experience and knowledge? For teams and small businesses, I provide consulting, classes, ...
Published work - Contact Bob - Who Dares Wins - Schedule
You shared this

Bob Mayer's Blog | WRITE IT FORWARD
writeitforward.wordpress.com/
Posted on November 19, 2011 by **Bob Mayer**. The last post was about the Kernel Idea. Let's look at some ideas. Character: "A housewife and female assassin ...
You shared this

Bob Mayer - Wikipedia, the free encyclopedia
en.wikipedia.org/wiki/**Bob_Mayer**
Robert **"Bob" Mayer** (born 1959) is an author, writing instructor, and former Green Beret. He has written over 30 titles under his name and his four pen names ...
Biography - Non-fiction books/series - Fictional books/series - References

Amazon.com: **Bob Mayer**: Books, Biography, Blog, Au...
www.amazon.com/**Bob-Mayer**/e/B000AQ1SUK
Visit Amazon.com's **Bob Mayer** Page and shop for all **Bob Mayer** books and other **Bob Mayer** related products (DVD, CDs, Apparel). Check out pictures ...

Bob Mayer - Google Profile
https://plus.google.com/101425129105653262515
Author at Self-employed - Psychology, United States ... NY Times Bestselling author, West Point Graduate.

What is cool about this is that Bob dominates the front page.

When we Google Area 51 we show up on the second page.

More videos for **area 51** »

All Proposals - **Area 51** - Stack Exchange
area51.stackexchange.com/
Area 51 is the Stack Exchange Network staging zone, where
users come together to build new Q&A sites. New site ideas are
proposed, discussed, and the best ...

UFOs? Aliens? **Area 51** Revealed - ABC News
abcnews.go.com › Technology
Apr 10, 2009 – Former insiders speak about one of the most
secretive military bases on Earth.

News for **area 51**

China's **Area 51**? Mystery desert patterns set web
tongues wagging
Sydney Morning Herald - 5 days ago
"It looks like our own **Area 51**," London's Daily
Telegraph newspaper quoted a user on Chinese
website Baidu as saying. **Area 51**, a US military base
in Nevada, ...
278 related articles

Area 51 eBook (book 1)
https://whodareswinspublishing.com/index.php?route...id=51
Former Green Beret Mike Turcotte, assigned to Nightscape,
security for **Area 51**, begins to realize things aren't as they
seem. Deep inside the Great Pyramid in ...
You shared this

Area 51, The Spear of Destiny and The taping of a SyF...
writeitforward.wordpress.com/.../area-51-the-spear-of-destiny-
and-th...
Mar 20, 2011 – We stopped at the Little Ale'Inn. Then I led them
out to the main gate to **Area 51**. We filmed for about an hour. I
was technically the 'expert' about ...
You shared this

Searches related to **area 51**

But we show up twice.

When we Google Who Dares Wins this is what we get.

Not the first listing, but on the front page.

And just to see if Jen Talty rocks the SEO.

Now these searches were using Firefox. When I did the same searches on Explorer on a PC, for the most part the results were the same, with the exception of Area 51. Bob's name or book did not come up until page 3.

Here is a good YouTube video that talks about snippets and search results: http://youtu.be/vS1Mw1Adrk0

Basic website design is written in HTML code. For example, Jen created Bob Mayer's site from scratch using HTML (http://bobmayer.org). HTML uses tags and for any page you have on the Internet you will have the <head> tag and there should be the title of your web page. A little trick with WordPress blogs: You don't have to use your name as the URL. We didn't for Write It Forward because the use of the word Write is searched for more often than Bob Mayer. However, by utilizing the name of the blog as Bob Mayer's Blog, it doesn't matter if you look for Bob Mayer or Write It Forward Blog, the blog comes up first.

Page title is important to SEO. You want to create unique tags for each page.

(Title SEO HTML tags look like this <title>Bob Mayer Home Page</title> This is how it shows up in Google.)

One of the things we can do better on both our business website and Bob's website is making better use of the description Meta tag. For now, we grab the first part of his home page. The SEO HTML tags looks like this <meta name="description" content="What can I do for you based on my experience and knowledge?">

The entire header would look like this
<html>
<head>
<title>Bob Mayer Home Page</title>
<meta name="description" content="What can I do for you based on my experience and knowledge?">
</head>
<body>

Now granted, this is if you are using HTML to write your website. If you are working with a template, then you want to make sure you use the right descriptors. Most good templates, including WordPress, give you places to write a title and a description. This is what search engines will grab. If you go to post a link and you don't get a description in Facebook or wherever you are posting, it's because there is no meta tag with the description associated to the that web page. If you have access to the HTML files you can locate the header and correct it.

Caveat: If you are using Word to create any kind of webpage, and you use the 'save as web page function,' the coding is an issue and this can affect your SEO.

There are other things such as URL Structure. You want to use words and you can't have spaces so do things like http://BobMayer.org/Bio or http://bobmayer.org/WDW_Writers.html so that the URL makes sense.

If you change a page name or even change websites or have more than one domain, but only use one website, you want to do what is known as a redirect. We did this when we redid Bob's website and got rid of http://bobmayer.org/blog so that anyone who had his blog bookmarked was automatically redirected to the new Write It Forward blog. (Jen just checked to make sure it was still working, and it is.)

SEO for mobile phones is becoming a huge issue. Many sites on the Internet are not set up to function well on smartphones. This is an issue we are currently working on at Who Dares Wins Publishing.

Side Note: There is now a feature on your WordPress blog to create a swipe image on the iPad. Jen did one for Write It Forward, but the image size (even though we used their specs) didn't convert properly. If you have an iPad, you can go to the Write It Forward Blog and you will see what we mean.

Analytics

We spent a few hours talking with Hubspot about maximizing our search potential and making better use of the information flowing in and out of our website. Who is coming to visit? Where are they coming from? And where are they going? Honestly, you can drive yourself nuts with this information, but it is important.

For the average author you want to know if people are visiting your website from Facebook, Amazon, B&N and other sites. In return, you want to know where they are clicking out of. The links you have on your website are very important because they are a call to action. One of the things we do is put up links to Barnes and Noble and Amazon for customers who would prefer to buy our books from those sites. People are loyal to these eBookstores, and while those same customers are also loyal to our authors, we give them the option as a courtesy.

We track where people are coming from when they visit the blog. This gives us information about how our presence marketing is working. The majority come from Twitter, Facebook and Yahoo groups. It also gives us information about who is "talking about us." We've found ping backs to forums we've never heard of discussing what we are doing on Write It Forward. When we join and comment, we are building a larger community.

All of this is important because the Internet is huge and it's just getting bigger, and more and more authors are putting their footprint on it. There needs to be a balance between how much time you spend developing quality metadata, securing SEO and analyzing the data coming in and out of your sites. Don't forget, there will be marketing and promotion that needs doing and of course, writing the next book.

Direct Sales, Hand Sales, and Apps

Direct Sales

One mode of sales that is rarely discussed is direct digital sales from the author to the reader. At Who Dares Wins Publishing, we set up our website so that it accepts credit cards and automatically sends the book to the purchaser in the correct format. This required two things: accepting credit cards and automating the website.

Frankly, while we do sell books, the reality is most people go with their known online bookstore, whether it's Amazon, Barnes & Noble or wherever. It's the McDonald's syndrome where people prefer the known over the unknown. Still, it generates more than enough income to have paid for the construction and operating cost and we make almost 100% royalties off sales. It's also convenient to be able to take credit cards, especially for our online courses at Write It Forward.

Hand Sales

If you have your book in POD, then you can sell it directly to the consumer. We find this works quite well at conferences and conventions with our non-fiction that is aimed at the people attending. Even better, sales really go up after one of us speaks.

We've found some tricks of the trade. During a keynote, Bob will place copies of his books on the table in the room with "Review Copy Don't Remove" stickers. This allows people to actually see and look through the book. Which leads to trick #2. Put it in their hand. If doing a book signing, hand the book to the person standing in front of your table. People are more apt to buy something they have in their hand, than something on the table.

Accept credit cards. We have a device that will swipe a credit card to the iPhone. People are much more willing to pay with credit card than check or cash.

Give back. At conferences, we will often ask the people running the conference to give us a volunteer to sell our books and in exchange we will give 20% of our gross back to the conference. This accomplishes two things: it frees us to present, while making the books available for sale. And it makes us more attractive speakers as we give back to the conference a portion of our sales.

Apps

A trend is for authors to get their own apps. This can be expensive and unless you are a brand name author, not very useful. People are swamped with apps and loading one exclusive to you as an author is doubtful. However, if you can have a dynamic app that is constantly updated, it might work. There is no doubt someone will have great success with an app as an author, but for 99%, it's a waste of time and money.

AUDIO BOOKS

This is a large market and one not many authors are fully exploiting, especially self-published authors. The Audible ACX program is extremely easy to use. You claim the rights to your book, and then create a profile. Be sure the product description is exactly what you want (similar to what will appear on your Amazon page for the book) because getting it changed is very difficult. There are two ways to proceed. You can do a 50-50 split with the production talent on royalties, thus not having to pay up-front. Of course, this means the talent believes the title will sell enough copies to make it worth their time. This is something you have to pitch to potential producers in the comments section. Or, if you have confidence and the funds, you can pay up-front and you get all the royalties. Since a 100,000 word book will cost you between $1,500 and $2,000 to get produced, if not more, this means you are looking for a long-term recoup of your investment.

If you go exclusively with Audible, your royalty rate starts at 50% and then has an escalator once you pass 500 copies sold, all the way to 90% if you sell a lot. Also, Audible prices books according to the length of time. A 100,000 word book is around 10 hours so the price is just over $20. Thus, each copy sold nets you around $10. You can do the math to see which production option is best for you.

You post your book along with an audition excerpt for the talent to read. This excerpt should be short, maybe a page or two, and include something where there is dialogue to see how the talent handles that. You then get auditions and listen to them. If you "like" an audition you can make an offer. Once an offer is accepted you set a time for the first fifteen minutes to be delivered and approved, and then for the entire book. It is a slow process, but you can get a book live within one month depending on the talent's schedule.

Unless you are a professional, we do not recommend doing your own book. Just like you have to pay for quality editing, you have to pay for a quality audio book.

Bob Mayer and Jen Talty

SECTION FIVE: THE FUTURE

It's a great time to be an author!

Bob Mayer and Jen Talty

THE FUTURE OF AUTHORS

The printed book will become "retro," like CDs and LPs before downloads, but the book will not die. Readers will still exist and they will download their favorite authors and enjoy stories on their eReaders just as they did while holding the printed book in their hands. The basic concept of the story will not change. How we read them might change, but the main job of the author to entertain the reader will never change.

However, as technology gives us more options, we have to learn how to use them. A key buzzword gaining traction is "transmedia,"which is telling the same story across different media: book, game, film, etc. Because the media are different, the story will actually change somewhat. Publishing is one of the last of the media to embrace change. So right now, this isn't that important, but in the next couple of years, the ability to incorporate story into transmedia will change things.

In a nutshell, transmedia storytelling is a process that integrates elements of fiction across multiple delivery channels. The end product is supposed to be a unified and coordinated entertainment experience.

This is something that Bob Mayer and Who Dares Wins Publishing will be actively pursuing in the coming years.

Imagine, for a moment, being able to sit back and enjoy Bob Mayer's nine-book series, *Area 51*. Imagine then being able to open up your Area 51 app and join Mike Turcotte in the battle against Alien forces, or perhaps go inside Kelly Reynolds' mind as she communicates with main computer. And since you haven't really had enough, you turn on your Xbox or PS3 and battle it out live.

Or if you are a history buff and have been reading *Duty, Honor, Country A Novel of West Point and the Civil War* and are now hooked on the Duty, Honor, Country Graphic Comic series on your iPad.

Storytelling across multi-media, while still in its infancy, is going to be one of the waves of the future. Being prepared for what is coming is the only way to succeed at where you are now.

Another difference in the 21st Century author compared to the previous century is the author has more control over the success of their career. There are more choices for authors today than in the past and we don't see that changing. Authors will always have the option to seek traditional publishing or they can self-publish without the negative branding that used to go with it.

Five years ago, Jen argued that it wasn't just the publishers that needed to change, but it was the authors that needed to change the way they think and do business. Advances are shrinking. That is a fact. Print runs are getting smaller. Fact. Print distribution to the stores that do sell physical books are based on the top 10% of publishing. Fact. If you want to survive in publishing you have to adapt. This means being willing to take calculated risks. When Bob went to Amazon to discuss a possible joint venture with some of his books it wasn't about the "advance," though five years ago, it would have been. Today it's about product placement and making the direct connection to the readers.

The concept of profit sharing rather than paying an advance will begin to dominate publishing. We don't do advances at Who Dares Wins Publishing. Entangled, a new romance publisher, is employing the same policy.

The role of the author is more than writing and promoting. The role of the author is running a business and everything that encompasses. It doesn't really matter what road you wish to take, what matters is how you plan on getting there. In the past, writers could rely on their agents and publishers to run the "business" part (to an extent, but if you read Write It Forward, you'll learn that an author must always be in charge of their career). Today, authors really need to know how to run a business. By gaining more control of our careers, we also gain more responsibility. The 21st century author is one that is aware of all aspects of their "author business."

We have always said Content is King. Writing is our first priority. Without story, we have nothing to go forth and either sell to New York, or promote on the Internet. A lot of things are going to happen over the next ten years in publishing, but two things will remain the same. Writers will write. Readers will read.

The successful authors will be those who stay ahead of the changes rather than react to them.

THE FUTURE OF PUBLISHING

The magic eight ball, when asked, "What is the future of publishing?" responds with... *ask again later.* We don't know. We can make predictions, but don't really know what tomorrow will bring. Five years ago, no one thought eBooks would be such a big deal. Now we're talking enhanced eBooks, and you can't turn on the TV anymore without seeing either James Patterson or Jane Lynch pimping the new Nook Tablet.

More and more authors are self-publishing and with great success. And some of these authors are signing deals with New York traditional publishers. Editors are combing the eBook bestselling lists looking for self-publishing diamonds. So are agents, who are also becoming "assisted publishers," helping their clients either publish backlist, or to publish books New York didn't want.

While print distribution continues to shrink, the global market is expanding. iBooks now has 32 stores. Amazon has six stores and is still expanding. We've loaded a German edition of *Bodyguard of Lies* and a Spanish Edition of *Area 51* to all platforms. We loaded a Spanish Edition of *An Unusual Journey Through Royal History* and have a translator currently working on Spanish Edition for the first book in the *Atlantis* Series. We are putting many of our books into Audio.

The publishing industry is facing the need to embrace and adapt to the growing technology. This is not going to be any easy task. It will take time and many growing pains for the industry. Authors are going to struggle, as the midlist has pretty much disappeared in traditional publishing.

Authors may not like the idea of a no-advance business model, but if publishers can work out a more equitable profit sharing agreement, that gives the author more incentive to promote and build their audience. However, the trend right now is, low advance, low print run, and no marketing. The flaw isn't in the low advance, it's in the focus on print run. We've seen authors hit the *NY Times* list with eBooks. (Lisa Gardner and CJ Lyons have both done it.)

The shift is happening, but it's very slow going in such a large business. New York publishing is going to hit a few more bumps, but the future for authors is a bright one. Readers will always want a good story and READERS RULE.

In Closing

It's the Wild West right now in Publishing and it's going to keep changing and shifting as the eBook market continues to grow. The only thing we know for sure is that to succeed you have to focus on the craft of writing (your product) and the business of publishing (how to get product to readers).

While it is a scary time in publishing, it truly is an exciting time for authors. We have more control of our careers than ever before. Technology has created a direct line between us and our readers like never before.

Let's restate the salient points we began this book with:

1. In it for the long haul, rather than thinking you're playing the publishing lottery. We see way too many writers who want success *now*. They check sales figures every day. Instead, they need to think about perhaps succeeding in 3 to 5 years with at least a half-dozen titles under their belt.
2. Plan for the long haul. At **Who Dares Wins Publishing** we're looking at least three years ahead. We have a writing and production schedule laid out that keeps us on task.
3. Stay one step of ahead of the trends. Act, don't react. This means sometimes you must take risks. Many of these attempts will fail, but those who succeed will be on the front end of the trends.
4. Write good books. This one seems so basic, but we see too many writers spend so much more time worrying about promotion instead of worrying about the quality of their craft. Bob has learned more in the last two years about writing than in his first twenty.

5. Sweat equity. This ain't easy. It never has been. We've followed the careers of many writers. The majority of writers who are having the most success as indies have a backlist, which is the sweat equity from the time they spent in the trenches in traditional publishing. For a new author, you have to create this sweat equity.

6. Run an efficient business. Most writers just want to write. They don't want to deal with all the details of running a business, but being an indie author means you are self-employed. We know people who were great doctors or lawyers but went bankrupt because they couldn't run their business.

7. Networking and team building. "Indie" is an interesting term because in fact, we believe it's very difficult to succeed on one's own. You're going to need help with the books (editing, covers, formatting, etc.) and you're going to need help with the promoting.

8. Build a platform that has a specific message. At Write It Forward we view our platform as being author advocates. We see too many writers whose platform seems to be "buy my book". People have to have a reason to read your blog, RT your tweets, listen to you.

9. Stay informed. The industry and technology are changing fast. Many people are trying a lot of different things. Some will work, some will fail. But staying up to date on everything that's happening can help you make informed decisions.

10. Be assertive but not obnoxious. We've grown much more assertive in the past six months. One of the largest mistakes Bob made coming out of Special Forces and going into traditional publishing was trusting that other people would do their jobs without having to look over their shoulders. This cost him. Now he pushes others, gently, but consistently, in order to achieve goals.

In sum. Writers, your fate is in your hands now.

Lead, Follow, Or Get The Hell Out of The Way...

Bob Mayer and Jen Talty

APPENDIX A

List of Internet Resources

AUTHOR INFORMATION

Bob Mayer
http://bobmayer.org

Jen Talty
http://jentalty.com

Write It Forward
http://writeitforward.wordpress.com

Write It Forward Workshops
https://whodareswinspublishing.com/WIF_Workshops.html

Who Dares Wins Publishing
http://whodareswinspublishing.com

PUBLISHING RESOURCES

Bowker--ISBN
http://myidentifiers.com

Kindle Direct Publishing (Amazon)
http://kdp.amazon.com/self-publishing/signin

Barnes and Noble PubIt
http://pubit.barnesandnoble.com

iTunesConnect
http://itunesconnect.apple.com

Kobo
http://kobo.com

Smashwords
http://smashwords.com

Vook
http://vook.com

LuLu
http://lulu.com

Lightning Source
http://lightningsource.com

COVER ART WEBSITES

iStockphoto
http://istockphoto.com

Shutterstock
http://shutterstock

SOCIAL MEDIA AND PROMOTION

Twitter
http://twitter.com

Facebook
http://facebook.com

Goodreads
http://goodreads.com

LinkedIn
http://linkedIn.com

Kindleboards
http://kindleboards.com

Nookboards
http://nookboards.com

Pinterest
http://pinterest.com

OTHER RESOURCES

Special Operations Warrior Foundation
http://www.specialops.org

Shawguides--Conference locator
http://shawguides.com

NY Times article on how Amazon is rapidly growing
http://www.nytimes.com/2011/10/17/technology/amazon-rewrites-the-rules-of-book-publishing.html

Bob Mayer and Jen Talty

Bob Mayer and Jen Talty

Bob Mayer and Jen Talty

CPSIA information can be obtained at www.ICGtesting.com
Printed in the USA
LVOW092156280312

275164LV00009B/122/P

9 781935 712862